MAKING
SOFT TOYS
FOR CHILDREN

Other books by Pamela Peake:

Creative Soft Toymaking Collins 1974
How to make Dinosaurs and Dragons Collins 1976
The Complete Book of Soft Dolls David and Charles 1979
Catcraft Collins 1984
The Book of Toy Making Ebury Press 1986
Learn to Make Soft Toys WI Books 1987
Little Grey Rabbit's Pattern Book Collins 1988

MAKING
SOFT TOYS
FOR CHILDREN

PAMELA PEAKE

PHOTOGRAPHY BY THE LONG ROOM STUDIO

DRAGON'S
WORLD

To my mother, Nyola Warnes

Dragon's World Ltd
Limpsfield
Surrey RH8 0DY
Great Britain

First published by Dragon's World 1988
Reprinted 1991

Art Director Bob Gordon
Editor Mirren Lopategui
Managing Editor Pippa Rubinstein

British Library Cataloguing in Publication Data
Peake, Pamela
    Making soft toys for children.
    1. Soft toys. Making – Manuals
    I. Title
    745.592'4

ISBN 1 85028 029 0

Typeset by Florencetype Ltd, Kewstoke, Avon

Printed in Portugal

D.L.B.-37.957-88

CONTENTS

INTRODUCTION

Making toys is an activity that for many continues throughout life. For children there will always be play with custom built toys provided by indulgent parents, but there are times when these are turned aside in favour of toys that they have fashioned for themselves from whatever is at hand. Such early creativity lays the foundation for future skills and should always be encouraged.

Schoolchildren gain further experience when they make papier mâché puppets for shows, build boats and wheeled toys in the workshop, learn to knit and sew in the studio, as well as an understanding of aerodynamics with paper darts.

For parents and grandparents there is often a return to toymaking after a break of some years. Being able to enjoy making toys successfully is very satisfying—it brings all manner of rewards, not the least of which is seeing the delight that it brings to children and the happy memories of your own childhood that it will undoubtedly evoke.

GENERAL INSTRUCTIONS

This is a book about making soft toys for children and consequently the emphasis is on suitability, durability and play value rather than on making exotic, exhibition toys or toys with so-called advanced techniques like jointing or wiring. All the toys are made from easy-to-find fabrics and generally follow a basic cut, sew and stuff sequence of construction. There are over forty different patterns for you to choose from and these have been arranged in four sections—nursery time favourites (toys for the very young), dolls, animals and dressed animals.

Each toy is complete with its own colour picture, shopping list, pattern, cutting guide and step-by-step instructions for putting it together. In addition the toys have been colour-coded according to the number of skills needed to make them which in turn reflects the degree of difficulty. Experienced toymakers will be able to start anywhere while those new to toy-making or with few sewing skills should keep to the toys suggested for beginners while they gain experience.

All the basic know-how needed for making the toys is to be found in this section. Read it carefully before starting and refer back to it from time to time as necessary. Problems usually arise from not fully understanding a technique or using the wrong materials. Follow the instructions carefully, therefore, and you should have much pleasure in making your toys just like those illustrated.

THE SKILLS LEVEL

Have you ever looked at a toy pattern and wondered whether you would be able to make it? Well, now the guesswork has been removed for all the toys have been colour-coded according to the degree of difficulty and skills needed for construction. Look for the colour-coding before you begin and then you will know what to expect. There are three ratings, green, blue and red.

Of course, all this is relative for some toys may be borderline between two ratings and what may be considered difficult for some could be only moderately taxing to others. On the whole borderline ratings have been put into a higher category so that green really means easy and red is for the experienced toymaker.

GREEN   This is the pattern to use if you are new to toy-making with few sewing skills or do not have a lot of time. It will generally use
○ few main pattern pieces
○ easy to sew fabrics
○ plain sewing
○ a simple shape to stuff
○ simple clothing
○ few extras or details to add

THE SKILLS LEVEL

NURSERY TIME FAVOURITES

Robbie Rabbit
Scamp
The Acrobats
Activity Blocks
Happy Hippos
A Baker's Dozen
Ball Games
Baby Blackface
Percival Trotter
Sweet Dreams

DOLLS

Gingham Girls
Loose Tubes
Pierrot
Able Seaman Ben
Yeoman Warder Hal
Baby Love
Baby Love's Carry Cot and Teddy
Global Children

BLUE This is the pattern to use if you are already familiar with toy-making and have a reasonable amount of time. It will generally use
○ more than six pattern pieces
○ two or more different fabrics
○ embroidery or yarn hairstyles
○ extras to be added
○ possibly new techniques

RED This is the pattern to use if you have plenty of experience and time. It will generally have
○ many pattern pieces, including some given as measurements
○ problem fabrics that require special handling such as velvet, long pile fur and stretch knits
○ challenging details
○ awkward pieces to fit carefully
○ plenty of extras
○ different stuffing requirements

ANIMALS

The Owletts
Little Blue
Selina Seal
Beshiung-chin
Bumbles the Bear
Gilbert the Gibbon
Dorinda Dragon

DRESSED ANIMALS

A Couple of Kittens
Abeargail
Edward and Edwina
Melissa Mouse
Harriet Hare
Brock the Badger

CHOOSING THE CORRECT MATERIALS

An appealing toy is the result of the right aesthetic combination of pattern, fabric, colour and finishing details. The fabrics listed have all been selected with the design in mind and consequently take into account such characteristics as colour, patterning, weight, texture, pile depth, stretch and, in the case of clothes, drapeability.

Close alternatives will always be acceptable and obviously you will choose a fabric that you like or perhaps are making do with what is available. Take care with alternative selections for it goes without saying that a doll made from a firmly woven fabric will be quite different in size from one made to the same pattern with a stretch fabric. Also, red and yellow Pandas become different animals altogether, not impossible perhaps but certainly questionable. Similarly, Gilbert in a short pile fur would lose all his charm and be boring and Snowball without his silky pile would not be so cuddly.

Remember that the length and width refer to the fabric recommended and that if you choose a different fabric it is quite possible that you will need a different amount.

A selection of furs that shows just some of the variety available to toymakers.

a. A very short pile fur with the appearance of velvet and a pile depth of 5mm (³⁄₁₆ in).
b. A short pile fur with a polished finish and a pile depth of 1 cm (³⁄₈ in).
c. A short pile fur with a matt finish. The pile depth is 1 cm (³⁄₈ in).
d. Simulated beaver, a dense short pile fur with a pile depth of 1.25 cm (½ in).
e. A coarse, medium pile fur with a pile depth of 2.5 cm (1 in).
f. Furnishing Dralon for paws and ear linings.
g. A long pile fur called Longhair. The pile depth is 5 cm (2 in) at least.
h. This shows the woven backing of a simulated spotted cat fur.
i. Spotted cat fur having a pile depth of 18 mm (¾ in).
j. This shows the knitted backing of a short pile fur.
k. Simulated badger fur showing one edge shaved off the 2.5 cm (1 in) pile.

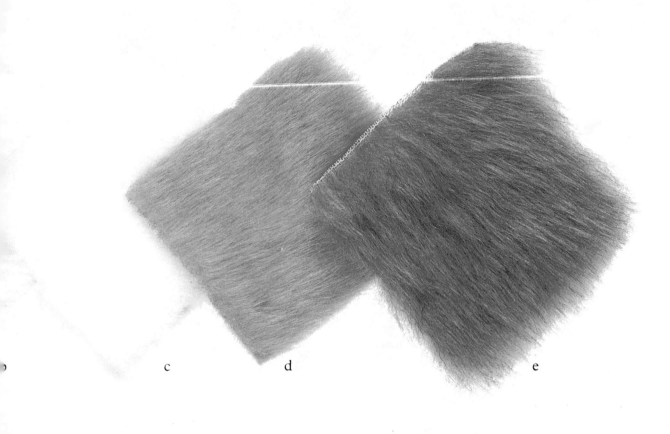

c   d   e

h   i   j   k

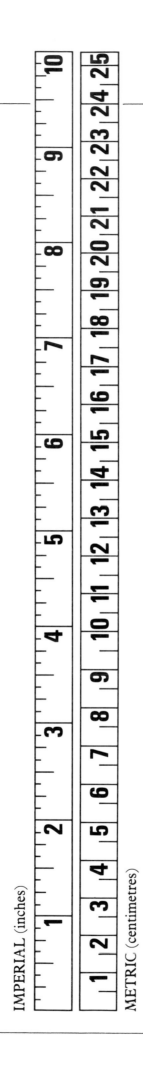

IMPERIAL (inches)

METRIC (centimetres)

QUANTITIES AND MEASUREMENTS

Measurements are given in both metric and imperial units, the latter being in brackets. Length is always given first followed by the width unless the measurements are for a square. You are urged to follow one system throughout as the two are not always direct conversions and are not therefore interchangeable.

Quantities are often rounded up and are consequently generous allowing for several different layouts and even a possible mishap when cutting out.

PATTERNS AND LAYOUTS

Patterns are the most important part of any toy for without them you cannot even make a start. Experienced toymakers can often work from the information given on the pattern alone and make their toys along well-established guidelines, checking with the photograph from time to time to confirm that they arc on the right track. It therefore makes good sense to spend time making an accurate copy and to understand all the markings.

You will find that the patterns for each toy have been reduced in size to fit comfortably together on a page and then overlaid with a grid of squares. The sizes of the squares in the grid are given in the scale and will usually be 5 cm (2 in). You will have to reverse the process and enlarge the pattern in order to make a toy that fits the measurements and materials needed, as given in the instructions.

Make yourself a re-usable grid by ruling up a large sheet of paper into 5 cm (2 in) squares or whatever the scale calls for. Dressmakers' graph paper is a ready-made alternative. Now lay a large sheet of tracing paper over the grid and then transfer the outline of each pattern from the book on to the grid, square by square.

Some symmetrical pattern pieces are shown as a half only with a direction to 'place on the fold'. These should be made full size by transferring detail on to a folded piece of tracing paper. In addition some patterns have shared outlines and are superimposed one on top of another on the grid, an example being the front and back body pieces of Gilbert the Gibbon (p. 112). Make separate patterns for each piece taking care to follow the correct outline. Now cut out tracings and glue on to a sheet of card. When dry, cut out the cardboard. The advantages of a card pattern are twofold: it enables you to use them over and over again as templates for drawing around and it removes the need to use pins.

Transfer all information and markings on to your new pattern.

Some patterns are simple shapes such as squares, rectangles, strips and circles and these are given as measurements in the Cutting Guide. You can either draw these directly on to the wrong side of the fabric before cutting out or make a card pattern ready for future use.

Each pattern piece is identified by the part of the body or clothing that it represents and will tell you how many times it must be cut and whether you need to cut two identical pieces or a pair. 'Cut a pair' means cutting a right- and left-sided piece. To do this you simply draw round the pattern template then turn it over and draw round it again for the second piece. Beware, a common mistake is to turn it around rather than over—this does not make a pair.

CHECKLIST FOR LAYOUTS

1 Collect together all the pattern pieces needed for each fabric.
2 Check the Cutting Guide for additional patterns that are given as measurements.
3 Prepare fabrics for layout by washing, pressing or backing as necessary.
4 Lay fabric flat on a table top, either doubled or opened out, according to the type of fabric being used and wrong side uppermost.
5 Mark direction of the pile stroke on the back of fur fabrics with a large pencilled arrow.
6 Position longest and widest pieces first followed then by largest.
7 Fit smaller pieces in the spaces.
8 Make sure that pairs are correctly positioned.
9 Check that arrows are all parallel to the selvedge or follow the stroke of the pile.
10 Note special layout requirements when cutting stretch fabrics. These are given in the Cutting Guide.
11 Note which pieces only need to be rough cut at this stage.
12 Check your layout one final time then make a sketch of it for future reference and proceed to cut out.

KEY TO THE PATTERN MARKINGS

Grain arrow	This indicates the straight grain, stripe, nap, pile or knit direction. Pattern pieces are laid on the fabric with the arrow lying parallel to the selvedge and for nap and pile fabrics the arrows must all point in the same direction. Felt does not have a grain, therefore the pattern pieces are not marked with an arrow.
Cutting line	Cut on the inside of the cutting line for an accurate pattern.
Sewing line	This is the line along which pieces are seamed together and darts are made.
Seam allowance	This is the area between the cutting line and seam line and is generally 6 mm (¼ in). All pattern pieces in the book have a seam allowance.
Fold line	This marks the centre of a pattern piece and should be placed against the folded edge of the tracing paper when enlarging to make a full size pattern.
Guide line	This is a placement line for top stitching, gathering, or attaching elastic, lace and hair.
Match points	Use to line up pieces when sewing.
Seam letters A B C	These are similar to match points and are often used with match points to clarify sewing sequences.
Eye position	This marks the position of the eye.
CF CB	Centre front and centre back.

Tools and accessories needed for toymaking. Reading from top to bottom and left to right: dressmakers' graph paper; tape measure; fabric scissors; work basket with lace, ribbons, sewing threads and embroidery cottons; embroidery scissors; lead pencil; vinyl facemasks; tailor's chalk; chalk pencil; hedgehog with glass headed pins; chopsticks; quick un-pick-it; bodkin; press studs; assorted sewing needles; squeakers; musical unit; rouleau loop turner; safety eyes and noses; hem marker

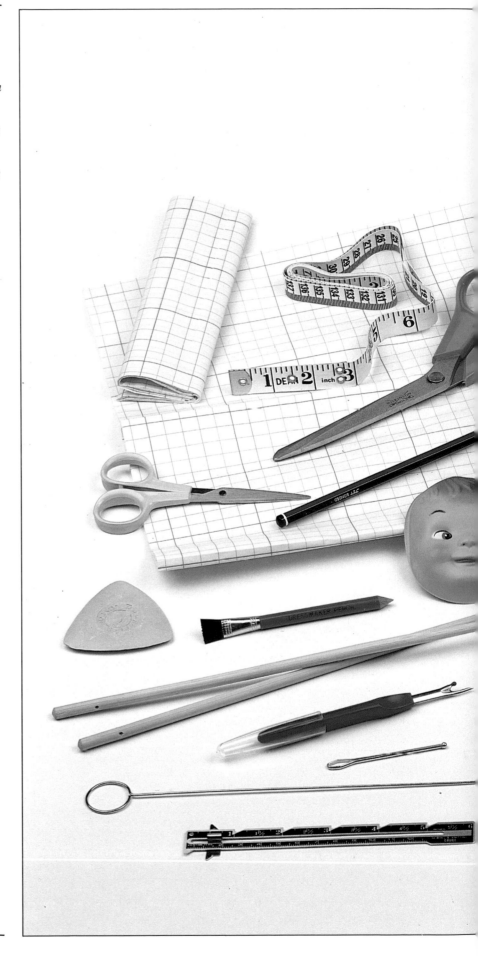

NEEDLES, THREADS AND STITCHES

Needles may be sharp or blunt and have large or small eyes. They may also be very short or several inches long. Each sewing method requires a particular kind of needle in order to work properly. Threads should pass through the eyes easily and not fray during sewing. Also the materials should not show holes when working. Whether sewing by hand or machine always use the finest needle possible.

You should have the following selection of needles available in your work box:-

Sharps for general sewing and handsewn seams
Crewel for embroidering details
Bodkin for threading elastic and ribbons
Darners for needle sculpture and reaching awkward spots
Ball point for handsewing knitted fabrics
Machine needles size 80/90 (11/14) for light weight fabrics
    size 90 (14) for velvet and heavy cottons
    size 100 (16) for fur fabrics

A polyester, cotton-covered thread has been used to sew all the toys and clothes. It is an all-purpose thread suitable for use with both natural and synthetic fabrics. Advantages are that it is easy to use, strong in the seams, won't shrink causing puckered seams after washing, has sufficient 'give' for sewing knitted stretch fabrics and is versatile—sewing all weights of fabrics with relative ease. It is a thread that can be used for both hand sewing and in the machine.

However, when it comes to closing seams and attaching heads, limbs, tails and ears to bodies a much stronger thread is required. Test the strength of the thread by trying to snap it in your fingers. Buttonhole twist, Bold stitch, linen upholstery threads and some crochet cottons will all generally pass this test and be suitable for use.

An invisible nylon thread makes super soft whiskers and is quite safe in the toys. (This thread is generally sold for soft furnishing rather than dressmaking so you may have to search for it.) Other details such as mouths and eyes, together with noses, are mostly embroidered with six-stranded embroidery thread using all six strands or just two or three strands for finer work.

A seam allowance of 6 mm (¼ in) is included on all pattern pieces except for a few that are cut from felt and these generally have a 3 mm (⅛ in) seam allowance. Extra allowance is provided for gather-

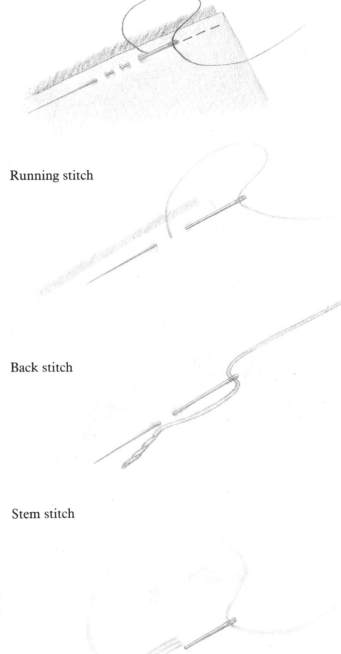

Running stitch

Back stitch

Stem stitch

Satin stitch

ing and hems. Seaming for all the toys and their clothes may be done on the machine or by hand, the choice is yours although some small and intricate piecing is best done slowly and carefully by hand. Whichever method of sewing you choose, the stitches will always be the basic stitches of plain sewing which you are probably already familiar with since childhood.

The sequence for sewing a toy together is given in the relevant step-by-step instructions, but it is important to know the basic methods of working that are common to all the toys. In general, pieces are sewn on the wrong side, with the right sides together. Basting, also known as tacking, is used to hold fabric together temporarily preparatory to sewing and is always preferable to pinning. When instructions tell you to baste, this will usually mean oversewing the edges of fur fabrics, tucking in the pile as you go and using a long running stitch for all other fabrics.

Sewing of seams may be by hand using a very tiny running stitch, or, better still, back stitch, and by using straight stitch on a sewing machine. Darts are made first then the parts of the body are assembled. Openings for turning and stuffing are left in inconspicuous seams wherever possible and preferably on straight edges. Before stuffing, the completed skin should always be checked for seam strength, clipped at the corners and along inside curves while points should be trimmed and outside curves notched.

Ladder stitch is used to close seam openings, attach heads and limbs and to brace spreading legs. It is essentially a running stitch worked on the surface and when finished, should be invisible. Always use a strong thread and start and finish by backstitching the ends away in a seam rather than by using a knot.

Herringbone stitch is used to close slashed openings where it is only necessary to bring the edges together. It is not invisible. All other stitches are decorative embroidery stitches and are used to work facial details, claws and just generally decorate a surface. The most frequently used are stem stitch, fly stitch, satin stitch and, less frequently, detached chain stitch and french knots.

Herringbone stitch

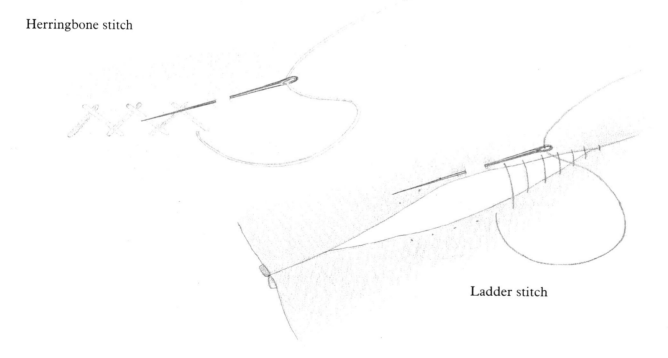

Ladder stitch

STUFFINGS AND FILLINGS

There are many different types and grades of synthetic fibre fillings which are suitable for stuffing the toys, the most successful and popular being the polyesters. Choose a good-quality white polyester which conforms to British Standards for health and safety. Such a filling will be lightweight, have a good bounce and in addition be clean to work with and washable.

Take the filling from the bag and tease out the fibres before stuffing it into the toys. Push down and out to the extremities first, using fingers, chopsticks or rods of almost any kind to pack it into position. Each toy will have its own stuffing requirements depending on whether it is to be a firm or softly filled skin. The relevant step-by-step instructions will tell you how to proceed.

Some of the toys are filled with 'beans' and these should be commercially produced plastic granules which again conform to safety standards. Traditionally bean bags have been filled with anything from rice to lentils and beans. If you use these food commodities then take the precaution to dry them thoroughly in the oven and be aware that these toys can't be washed.

Finally, some toys require sheet stuffing for parts of their bodies or for linings. Again, the preferred filling is a good-quality polyester batting.

SMALL-SCALE DRESSMAKING

All the dolls and some of the animals have a variety of clothes that are made using dressmaking skills with a slight difference. Because of their size, details like collars, pockets and setting in sleeves are often too difficult and have to be either eliminated or treated in another way.

Choose easy care fabrics that will launder well and can be kept clean. Polyesters have too much spring for the smaller clothes and are best passed over in favour of cottons with small prints.

Seams are generally not neatened in doll's clothes so you will have to allow extra if this is what you want to do. However in some instances you will see that a french seam is called for and in these cases an allowance has been made on the pattern.

All clothes should be fitted on the bodies as you are making them to check size and fit—likewise seams, turnings and such like should be pressed as you work, rather than left to the end. Most of the dresses are left open down the back and fasten with press snaps hidden under buttons. Half slips and panties have elasticated waists to help make the fit easier than a waistband. Awkward neck edges are simply neatened with bias strips which may either be purchased or cut in matching fabric.

Other edges like hems and sleeve openings are usually neatened with lace or hemmed before side seams are made. This is simply because it is easier to get at them when they are opened out flat. Sleeves are likewise easier to sew into armhole openings first, before the underarm seams are sewn. In these cases the underarm seams can continue into side bodice seams making small-scale dressmaking so much easier to do.

These are just general guidelines for you to follow and think about. More detailed instructions for making each item of clothing are covered in the relevant step-by-steps.

COMMERCIAL COMPONENTS

Safety eyes are the most frequently purchased
extras that toymakers will use. They are designed so
that, once correctly fixed in place, children will not
be able to pull them out of a toy. Safety eyes are
made in plastic and are produced in an ever increas-
ing range of styles, colours and sizes. Washers hold
them firm and these may be either plastic as well
or more usually metal. Most metal washers are
designed to be fixed with finger pressure only while
some have a lipped edge that requires a starlock tool
to lock them in place.

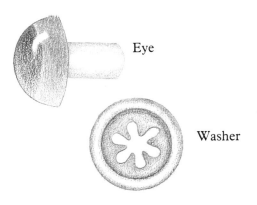

Eye

Washer

Your pattern marks an eye position and suggests
the size of eye most suitable for the character made
in the fabric listed. This position should always be
checked before inserting the eye as an alteration in
the seam allowance or a change of fur length and
even colour could affect the position.

Make a hole in the fur with an awl then push the
shank of the eye through from the right side to the
inside of the skin. Level the washer on the shank,
making sure that the teeth on the washer are facing
away from the back of the eye. Push down steadily
and firmly until it is pressed tight against the eye
with the skin fabric sandwiched between.

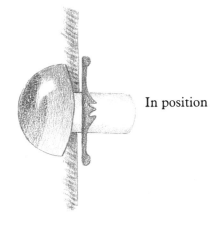

In position

Safety noses are fixed in the same way. In addition, some noses have a hole at the base of the shank
and this may be used to tie on a strong thread which
can then be stitched into place holding the nose firm
in position.

Other commercial components that are used less
frequently are vinyl face masks and all the noise
making units. Toys in the book incorporate musical
boxes with pull cords, chimes and squeakers while
Baby Love (p. 79) has a vinyl face mask that is
covered by fabric so that new, softer features can be
painted on with acrylic paints.

TRIMMINGS AND FINISHES

Frills, ruffs, ribbons, bows, lace and pom-poms are all to be found trimming the toys and adding greatly to their appeal. Detailed instructions for making them are given with the relevant toys but they are of course interchangeable. The bow around Scamp's neck (p. 29) is tied in a professional way and is invaluable when using ribbons that have a wrong and a right side.

Small, matching-sized bows are often more of a problem to make but like anything else not that difficult when you know how. Make a bowmaker tool for yourself by taking a piece of wood and knocking in two nails, the distance apart being the same as the required width of the bow. Take narrow ribbon behind both nails and cross over in front. Then take the upper ribbon between nails under the ribbon at the back then up and over back to the front again. Knot ends together tightly, slip ribbon off the nails and trim the ends neatly. All bows made on these nails will be the same size and are also virtually impossible to untie.

Now take time to look at your finished toy and attend to grooming. Check for loose ends, darning them in if necessary before cutting. Pick or brush seams to release any trapped fur and brush furs generally to tidy them up. Tug at limbs, ears, tails, wings making sure that they are all securely stitched in place. Likewise, tug at safety fixtures and whiskers to make sure that nothing is loose and on the move.

Is the general appearance good, is the stuffing smooth providing a good shape and does the toy stand well, balanced in the correct position? Do the legs splay out and need bracing by ladderstitching back to the body? Now is the time to attend to any faults and put them right.

It is also the time to reflect and note any alterations that you would like to make in future toys and to note any inspirational ideas that warrant experimenting with at a later date. Consciously think how you might interchange pattern pieces and come up with some designs of your very own.

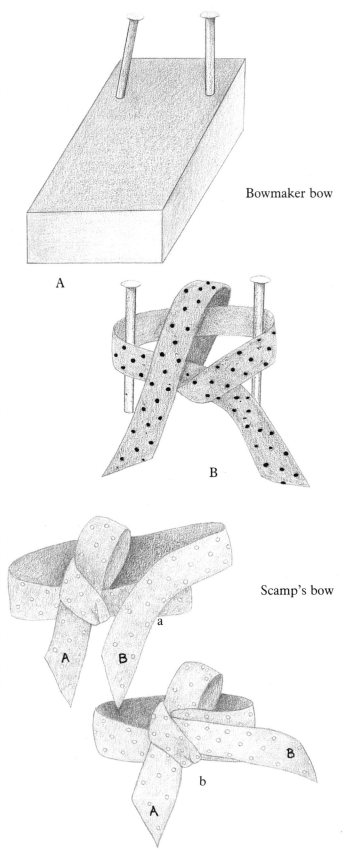

Bowmaker bow

A

B

Scamp's bow

a

A   B

b

A   B

NURSERY TIME FAVOURITES

The early years of childhood are a time of rapid development and change for youngsters when they are busy learning about themselves and the world that they live in. It is a time when play helps in interaction with others, laying the foundation for social skills. Toys are the tools of play and they can both educate and amuse.

Nursery Time Favourites consists of a collection of toys that will prove both entertaining and stimulating. There are toys to cuddle and talk to, colourful toys to look at and reach out for. Then there are toys that have hidden surprises like chimes and squeakers. Balls are toys that can be shared with other members of the family. Initially they will simply help with hand and eye coordination but later on they introduce youngsters to rules and team games. Textures, shapes and sizes are all taken into account; there is something for all stages of development in the pre-school years.

ROBBIE RABBIT

*What could possibly be easier than this little rabbit to
start you off on a successful toy-making adventure.
Robbie is disarmingly simple to make as he is
ingeniously constructed from little more than a square,
a circle and simple shaped ears.*

MATERIALS NEEDED

33cm (13in) square of unpolished,
   short pile fur
5m (5 yards) soft, white babywool
   fur tail
A pair of 14mm amber safety eyes
26g (1oz) stuffing
Embroidery thread for nose.

Height of Rabbit 15 cm (6in)

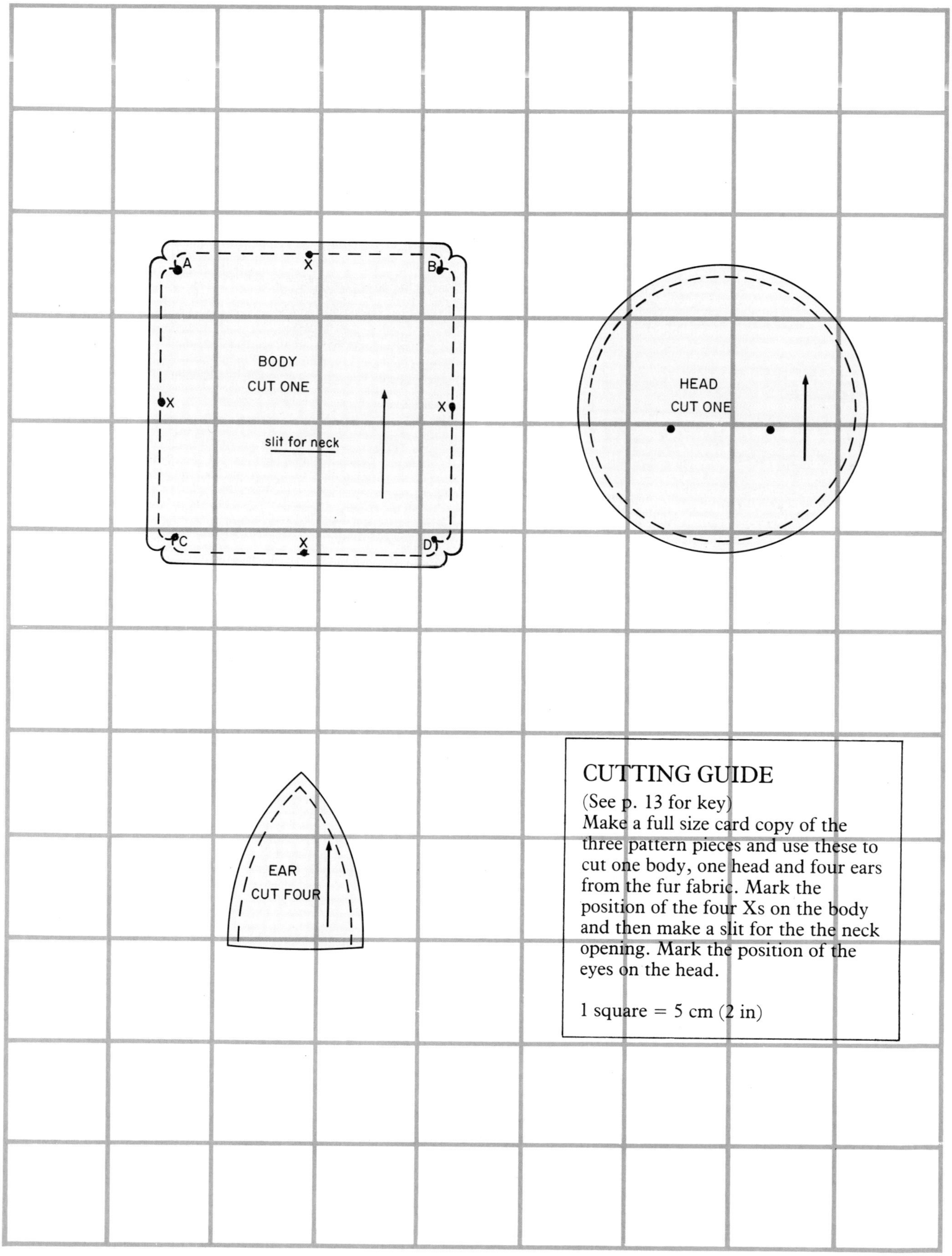

BODY
CUT ONE

slit for neck

HEAD
CUT ONE

EAR
CUT FOUR

CUTTING GUIDE
(See p. 13 for key)
Make a full size card copy of the
three pattern pieces and use these to
cut one body, one head and four ears
from the fur fabric. Mark the
position of the four Xs on the body
and then make a slit for the the neck
opening. Mark the position of the
eyes on the head.

1 square = 5 cm (2 in)

MAKING THE BODY

1 Fold the body square diagonally from A to D with right sides together. Sew from A to X to make a back leg. (See Fig. a).

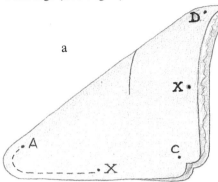

a

2 Now refold body and sew from B to X on the adjacent corner to make the other back leg. This brings three Xs together at the top of the legs on the underside of the body.

Match the remaining X which lies between D and C, to all the the other Xs and this will automatically form the front legs on the remaining corners. Sew each one in turn.

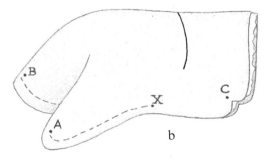

b

3 Turn completed bodyskin right side out through the neck slit. Insert a little stuffing into each of the legs in turn gradually filling them all and shape the body so that it stands securely with a definite front and back. Finish stuffing the body then close the neck by running a gathering thread around the slit and drawing up.

MAKING THE HEAD

4 Insert the eyes in the head then gather the edge with a strong, doubled thread. Pull on the gathers and enclose a ball of stuffing. Shape the head so that it is an oval with the gathers at the back. Insert more stuffing as necessary then fasten off the gathering thread.

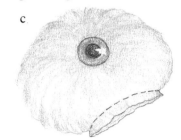

c

5 Position head on the front of the body so that the gathers and neck slit cover each other. Ladder stitch in place.

6 Sew two earpieces right sides together and repeat with remaining two pieces to make the second ear. Turn each ear right side out and fold in opposite directions to make a pair.

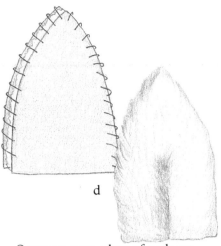

d

Oversew open edges of each ear in turn to hold the fold in place.

Ladder stitch ears to head working across the front first and then behind the ears to pull them back. The folded edges lie together on top of the head.

7 Embroider nose using all six strands, doubled. Work a long tailed fly stitch then finish with a straight stitch passed behind the end of the tail. This makes the mouth.

MAKING THE TAIL

8 Wind wool over three fingers approximately 65 to 70 times. Fasten off by tying securely in the middle. Fold bundle of wool in half and sew folded base with strong thread to make a one sided ball. Cut all the loops then sew tail to the body and finish by trimming wool to a pleasing, rounded shape.

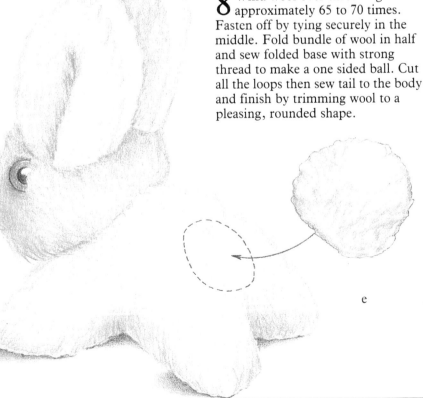

e

SCAMP

Puppies and youngsters have much in common with their playful antics. This little chap is easily made and could in fact be the start of quite a litter. Try colour changes and even different lengths of furs for greater variety.

MATERIALS NEEDED

31 cm × 62 cm (12 in × 24 in) wide
    short pile fur for body
31 cm (12 in) square of fur for ears
    and tail
56 g (2 oz) stuffing
A pair of 12 mm brown safety eyes
A scrap of black and red felt
51 cm (20 in) narrow ribbon for bow

Length of Dog 23 cm (9 in)

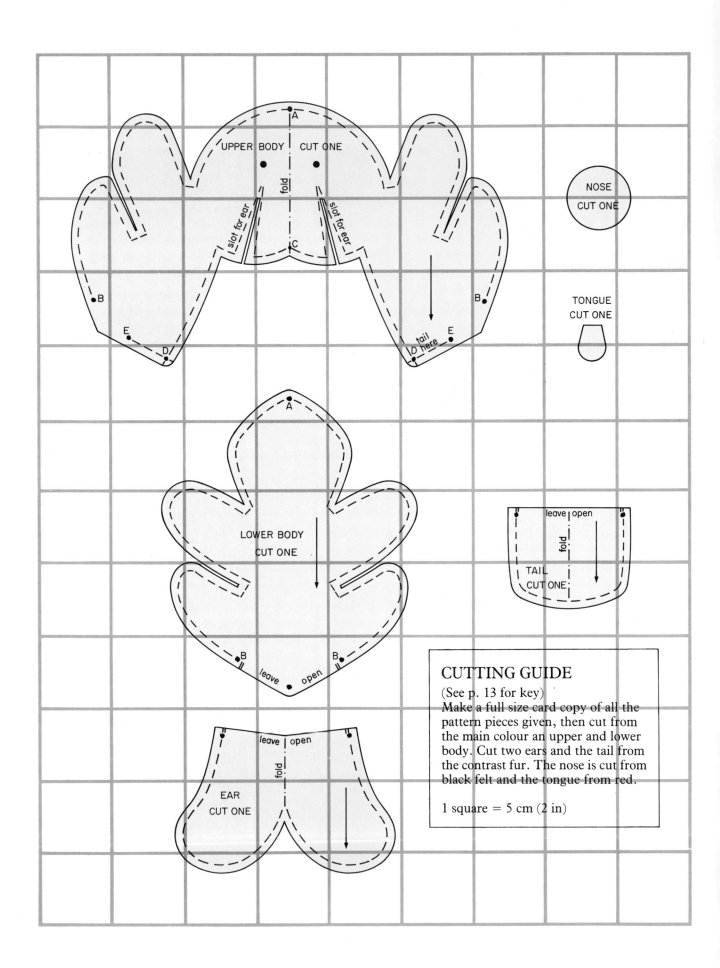

UPPER BODY CUT ONE

A

fold

slot for ear

slot for ear

C

B

B

E

E

D

D

tail here

NOSE
CUT ONE

TONGUE
CUT ONE

LOWER BODY
CUT ONE

A

B

B

leave   open

leave | open

fold

TAIL
CUT ONE

leave | open

fold

EAR
CUT ONE

CUTTING GUIDE

(See p. 13 for key)
Make a full size card copy of all the
pattern pieces given, then cut from
the main colour an upper and lower
body. Cut two ears and the tail from
the contrast fur. The nose is cut from
black felt and the tongue from red.

1 square = 5 cm (2 in)

1 Fold an ear in half and sew the curved edges together leaving the top open. Turn right side out and clean the seam. Make the second ear in the same way. Now place each ear in a slit on top of the head checking that they lie forward, framing the face. Sew in place. Fix the safety eyes in place.

2 Match upper and lower bodies together and, with the ears safely tucked out of the way, sew each side in turn together from A to B. Take care to square off between front and hind limbs, and between the neck and front limbs. Clip into corners. (See Fig. a).

3 Fold upper body in half lengthwise bringing raw edges together and seam from C to D. (See Fig. b). Fold tail in half and sew curved edge. Turn right side out and clean seam. Tuck tail into body and with raw edges level, seam D to E.

4 Turn completed body skin right side out and check now that ears are securely in place and that the limbs lie flat because the corners have been clipped correctly. Stuff the head, followed by limbs then the body. Ladderstitch the opening closed, easing in any fullness.

5 Gather the edge of the nose circle and enclose a small knob of stuffing as you pull up on the gathers. Fasten off securely making sure that the nose is a small, firm ball. Sew in position on the head. (See Fig. c). Sew tongue to the underside of the head with just the tip showing at the front.

6 The final touch is a bow tied around the neck and finished on the back of the head. Make a single knot in the ribbon at the required position. Form a loop with end A and then pass B in front of this loop to the back. Make a similar-sized loop with B then turn it back and feed the loop through the pass over in the front of the bow. Pull both loops tight and trim ends (See Fig. d; also p. 20).

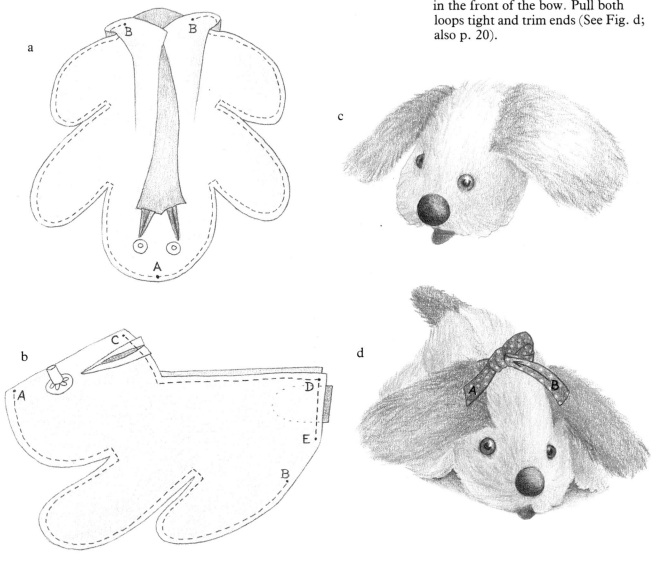

THE ACROBATS

A troupe of brightly coloured teds makes a colourful toy to tie across a pram or cot. Rearrange them as individual acrobats swinging and somersaulting through the hoops and you have the making of a circus mobile.

MATERIALS NEEDED TO MAKE 4 ACROBATS

23 cm × 150 cm (9 in × 60 in) wide tan stretch velour

56 g (2 oz) stuffing

Dark brown embroidery thread

3 thin plastic bangles

137 cm (54 in) of 3.75 cm (1½ in) wide red seersucker ribbon

46 cm (18 in) of 3.75 cm (1½ in) wide blue seersucker ribbon

46 cm (18 in) of 3.75 cm (1½ in) wide yellow seersucker ribbon

3 m (3¼ yards) of narrow striped ribbon for the ties

Height of each Acrobat 12cm (4¾ in)

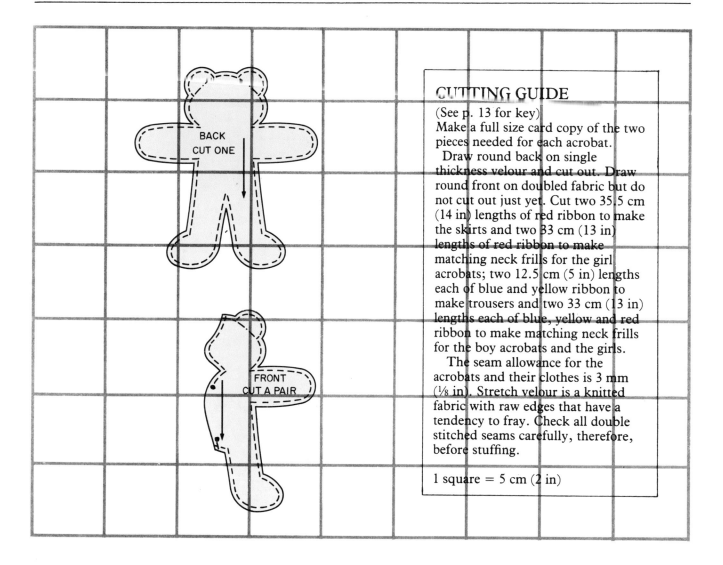

BACK
CUT ONE

FRONT
CUT A PAIR

CUTTING GUIDE

(See p. 13 for key)

Make a full size card copy of the two pieces needed for each acrobat.

Draw round back on single thickness velour and cut out. Draw round front on doubled fabric but do not cut out just yet. Cut two 35.5 cm (14 in) lengths of red ribbon to make the skirts and two 33 cm (13 in) lengths of red ribbon to make matching neck frills for the girl acrobats; two 12.5 cm (5 in) lengths each of blue and yellow ribbon to make trousers and two 33 cm (13 in) lengths each of blue, yellow and red ribbon to make matching neck frills for the boy acrobats and the girls.

The seam allowance for the acrobats and their clothes is 3 mm (⅛ in). Stretch velour is a knitted fabric with raw edges that have a tendency to fray. Check all double stitched seams carefully, therefore, before stuffing.

1 square = 5 cm (2 in)

MAKING THE BODIES

1 Hold both front body pieces together by pinning through the head and limbs. Sew centre front seam leaving it open between match points. (See Fig. a). Cut out shape and remove pins.

2 Sew front and back body together round outer edge and turn right side out. Work a tiny stab stitch across the base of each ear and through both thicknesses of velour. This stops the stuffing from entering the ears. Stuff the head, arms, legs and body in that order. Tie a double thread around the neck to hold the stuffing in place and to give the head more shape. Fasten ends off securely. Shape the tummy before closing the opening with ladder stitch. (See Fig. b).

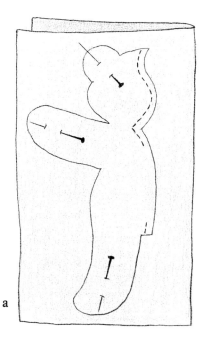

a

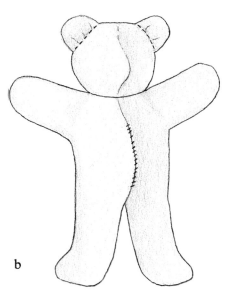

b

3 Use all six strands of embroidery thread and work blocks of straight stitches side by side for the eyes. The nose is a triangular block of straight stitches worked horizontally while the mouth is two single stitches sloping away from the base of the nose. Back-stitch embroidery thread around the neck groove to fasten off out of sight. Make three more acrobats.

MAKING THE CLOTHES

4 Seam the short ends of the trouser ribbon together then slip on to ted. Hold in place around the waist with a few small stitches. Oversew the edges together between the legs. Finish the trousers by sewing a short length of narrow ribbon to each leg with the join on the inside of the leg. (See Fig. c).

5 Seam short ends of neck frill ribbon together and then fold ribbon in half with seam hidden between the fold. Gather the folded edge and fit around neck. Pull up on gathering thread to draw in neck then fasten off. Dress second acrobat using other coloured ribbon.

6 Make neck frills for the girl acrobats in the same way as for the boys. Seam short ends of skirt ribbon together and gather to fit waist. A waist band for the skirt can be made using the narrow ribbon. (See Fig. d).

FINISHING OFF

7 The acrobats are joined together by stitching to the hoops. The girls at either end stand in the hoop which is then stitched to the back of their hands. The boys share the central hoop which sits tucked in their arms while the hands are stitched folded on to trouser fronts. The other hand of each boy is stitched securely to a girl's hand. (See Fig. e).

8 The remaining length of narrow ribbon is cut in half and each half is sewn to a girl's hoop, just behind her hand. The ribbons are used to stretch across the pram or cot and tie at the side.

ACTIVITY BLOCKS

Blocks are well-proven educational toys as they can provide many different challenges for developing youngsters. Soft blocks, in addition to aiding letter and number recognition, can incorporate other surprises. Hidden chimes and squeakers are fun to find and operate and different textures can be explored. Once you have made a basic block, many more ideas should occur to you.

MATERIALS NEEDED

Small pieces of fleece fabric
Small pieces of cotton prints with
   suitable pictures
Embroidery threads
Piping cord for tails
Chimes

Squeakers
A pair of 14 mm blue safety eyes for
   mice
Gingham to line ears
Felt for letters
112 g (4 oz) stuffing for each block

Size of each Block 10 cm (4 in) square

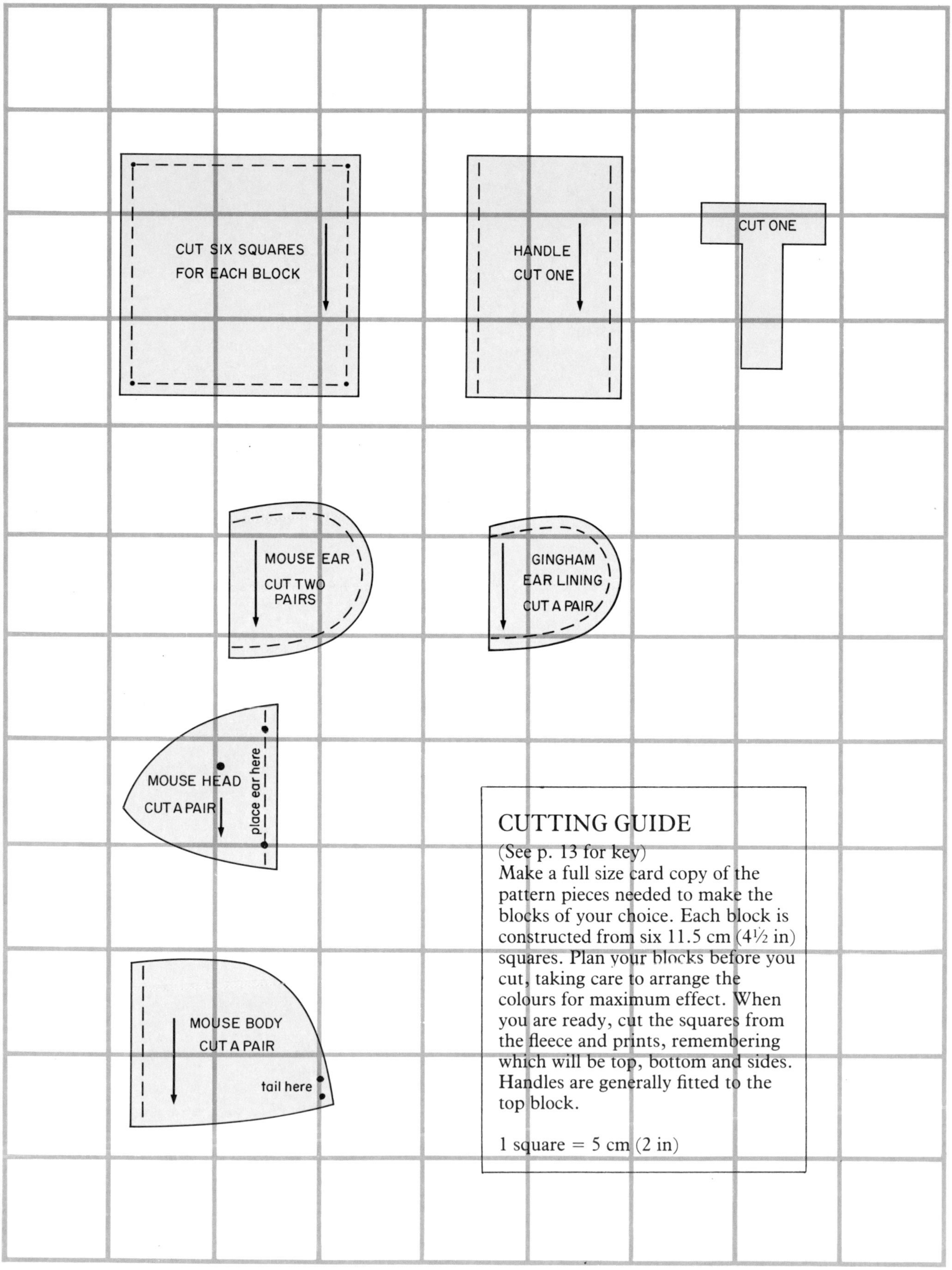

CUT SIX SQUARES
FOR EACH BLOCK

HANDLE
CUT ONE

CUT ONE

MOUSE EAR
CUT TWO
PAIRS

GINGHAM
EAR LINING
CUT A PAIR

MOUSE HEAD
CUT A PAIR

place ear here

MOUSE BODY
CUT A PAIR

tail here

CUTTING GUIDE

(See p. 13 for key)

Make a full size card copy of the pattern pieces needed to make the blocks of your choice. Each block is constructed from six 11.5 cm (4½ in) squares. Plan your blocks before you cut, taking care to arrange the colours for maximum effect. When you are ready, cut the squares from the fleece and prints, remembering which will be top, bottom and sides. Handles are generally fitted to the top block.

1 square = 5 cm (2 in)

MAKING THE CAT AND MOUSE CHIME BLOCK

1 You will need a blue handle, two blue, two red and two cat and mouse print or alternative print squares to make this block as well as a chime. Make the side walls first by sewing each print to a blue square then sewing the pairs together to make a strip of four. Lastly sew the strip together to complete the side walls. (See Fig. a).

2 Fold handle lengthways and sew. Turn right side out and sew at either end to the red top square. Fit top square into opening of wall and, with right sides together, sew all round. Take care to pivot the needle on the corners to make a perfect square.

3 Fit second red square into bottom of block and sew on three sides only. Turn block right side out. Wrap chime in scraps of soft fabric or even batting to mask the edges. Insert centrally into block and continue stuffing all round chime until block is full. Close opening with ladder stitch. (See Fig. b).

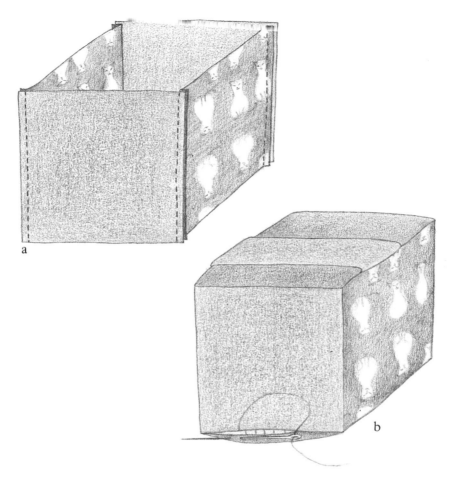

a

b

MAKING THE T FOR TEDDY BLOCK

1 You will need a red handle, two red, two yellow and two teddy print squares as well as a red felt letter T.

2 Topstitch the felt T to a yellow square then sew each yellow square to a teddy print square and complete the wall as outlined in the block above. Make a red handle and sew to the other yellow square. (See Fig. a).

3 Sew red top and bottom squares in place leaving an opening. Turn right side out, stuff and close.

a

MAKING THE MOUSE BLOCK

1 You will need six blue squares, white fleece mouse parts and eyes and tails to complete each mouse body. The ears have blue gingham linings and they each hide a squeaker.

2 Topstitch a mouse head to a blue square. Restitch over the edge with a close zig-zag stitch to cover the raw edges of the fleece. Fix a blue eye in place and embroider a nose and whiskers with three strands of pink embroidery thread. Make another head square in the same way but this time have the nose facing the opposite direction. (See Fig. a).

3 Topstitch then zig-zag a body to a blue square trapping the end of a 15 cm (6 in) length of piping cord in the tail position. Make a second body square in the same way with mice back to back and trap the other end of the piping cord under this body. Join both body squares together being especially careful to keep the shared tail free as a loop. (See Fig. b).

4 Gather the edge of a blue gingham ear lining and pull up to turn edge inwards. Topstitch gingham ear to the right side of a fleece ear lining. Sew this prepared ear lining to a plain fleece ear with right sides together. Turn ear right side out, insert a squeaker and sew ear to the back edge of a head square. Make and attach a second ear in the same way to the other mouse head.

5 Sew each head square to matching body square. (See Fig. c). Sew head squares together to make the wall then finish block by sewing top and bottom in place as outlined and stuffing before closing.

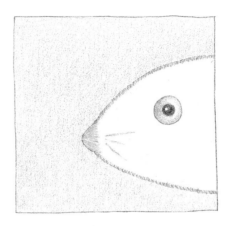

a

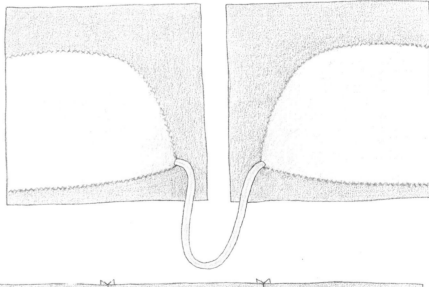

b

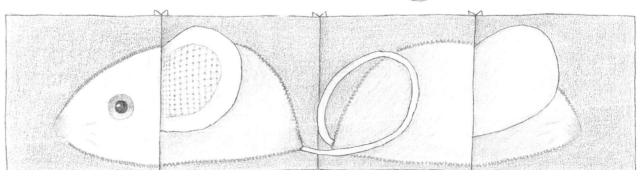

c

HAPPY HIPPOS

*A pair of Hippos filled with beans make a welcome change
from the more familiar green frogs. Likewise they are fully
poseable and will happily sit, stand or flop about for you
making a delightful duo.*

MATERIALS NEEDED

46 cm (18 in) square of short pile
   green fur
28 g (1 oz) stuffing
168 g (6 oz) dried rice
A pair of 16 mm safety eyes with
   green iris and moveable pupil
15 cm (6 in) square of green felt

Length of Hippo 20 cm (8 in)

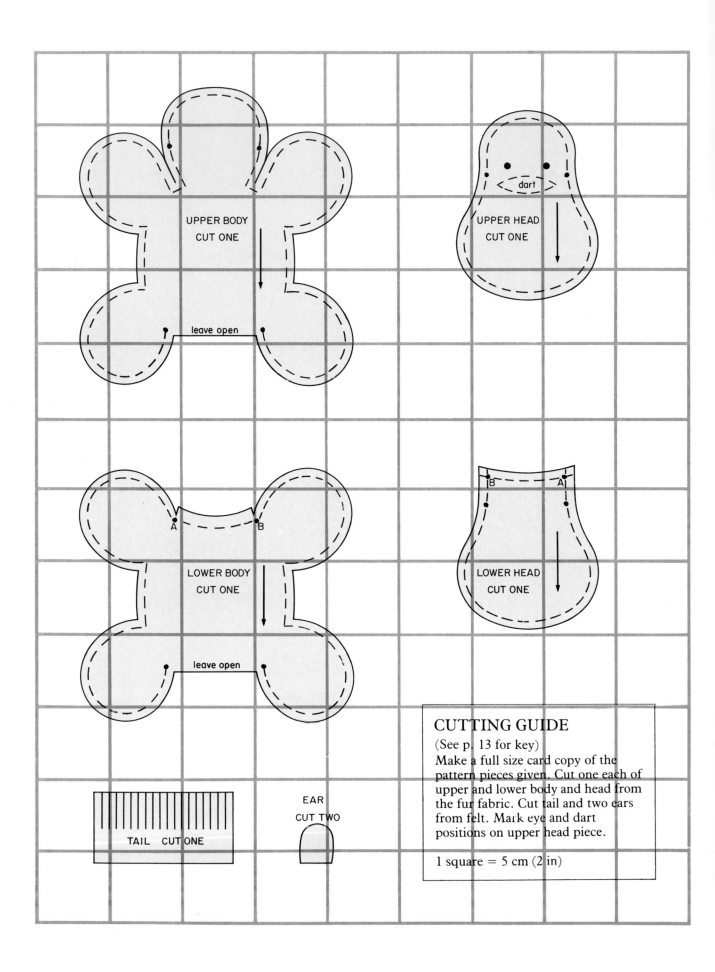

UPPER BODY
CUT ONE

leave open

UPPER HEAD
CUT ONE

dart

LOWER BODY
CUT ONE

A   B

leave open

B   A

LOWER HEAD
CUT ONE

TAIL   CUT ONE

EAR
CUT TWO

CUTTING GUIDE
(See p. 13 for key)
Make a full size card copy of the
pattern pieces given. Cut one each of
upper and lower body and head from
the fur fabric. Cut tail and two ears
from felt. Mark eye and dart
positions on upper head piece.

1 square = 5 cm (2 in)

1 With right sides together, sew lower head to lower body from A to B. (See Fig. a). Sew upper body to lower body and head on each side from match points on side of head around limbs to back opening between the hind legs. Clip corners at neck and between limbs.

2 Sew upper head to upper body around the crown from match points on either side. (See Fig. b). Fold upper head through centre of dart and sew. Take care to fold lower head out of the way.

3 Turn head right side out and fix eyes in place. Now turn the head back to the wrong side. Pin and tack upper and lower heads together around the snout easing in any fullness before sewing. Turn completed skin right side out and check that seams are secure and brushed clean before filling. (See Fig. c).

4 Fill snout with soft stuffing and remainder of body with rice. Ladderstitch the opening, pulling up on the stitches to draw the hind legs together. This gives Hippo more bulk on the rump. The soft stuffing in the snout can be held in place by anchoring a strong thread on the lower head and passing the needle up through the dart on the upper head and back to the start. Pull up on the thread to pull back of snout together then fasten off securely.

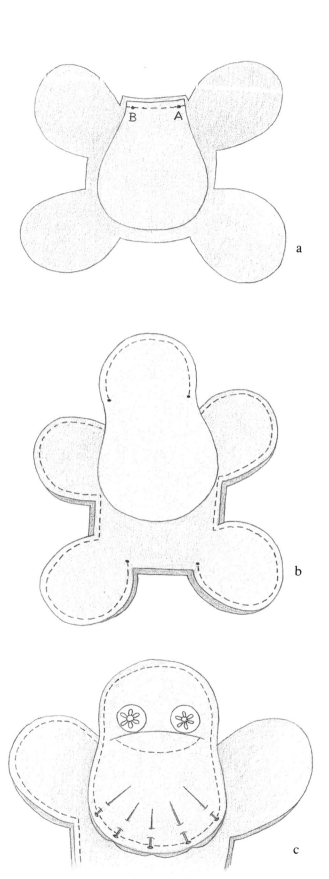

5 Fold ear in half and oversew bottom edges together to hold the fold. Make second ear in the same way but fold to opposite side to make a pair. Sew ears securely in place on crown. (See Fig. d).

6 Roll felt strip for tail into a tight coil and hem end in place. Sew tail to top of rump so that it isn't squashed when Hippo sits down. (See Fig. e).

d

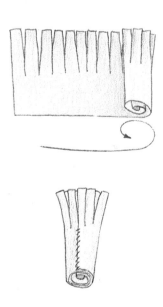

e

A BAKER'S DOZEN

*Take some brightly coloured fabric remnants and follow the
instructions for making these ingeniously designed oriental bean
bags which are known by the Japanese as Ote-dama bags.
Bean bags are used by children worldwide as non-bouncing
balls for playing games of Catch and Spot the Target.*

MATERIALS NEEDED

Remnants of firmly woven, brightly
  coloured cotton prints
Dried rice, birdseed, beans or pulses
  for filling
Each bag requires approximately
  56 g (2 oz) of filling

Size of Bag approximately 7.5 cm
(3 in) square

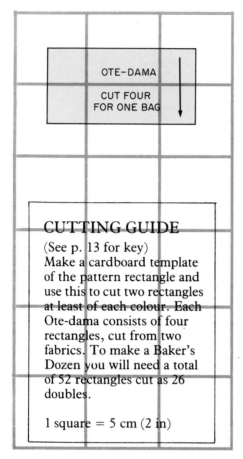

OTE-DAMA

CUT FOUR
FOR ONE BAG

CUTTING GUIDE

(See p. 13 for key)
Make a cardboard template
of the pattern rectangle and
use this to cut two rectangles
at least of each colour. Each
Ote-dama consists of four
rectangles, cut from two
fabrics. To make a Baker's
Dozen you will need a total
of 52 rectangles cut as 26
doubles.

1 square = 5 cm (2 in)

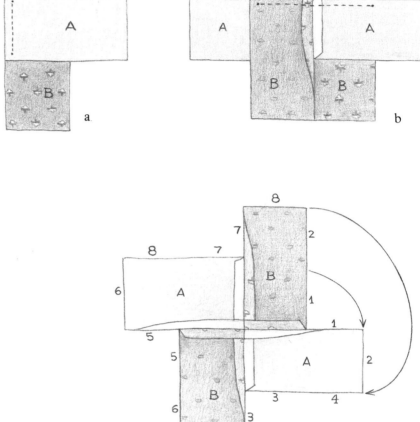

a

b

c

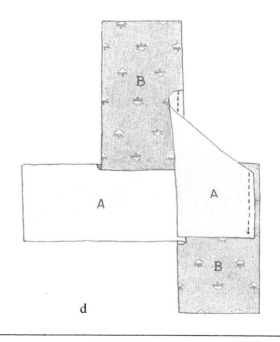

d

1 Sort fabrics into contrasting
colours then make each bag as
follows. Place colour A at right
angles across colour B and seam as
shown, leaving a small opening at
each end of a narrow seam. Sew
remaining two rectangles together in
the same way. (See Fig. a).

2 Join pairs together with seams
finger pressed open and
matching, again leaving a small
opening at each end of the seam. (See
Fig. b). Open partially completed
Ote-dama out flat and carefully note
the order of sewing that must be
followed to make the bag. (See Fig. c).

3 Bring adjacent edges marked 1
together and sew. Take care to
form neat corners without tucks or
puckers that would spoil the
symmetry. (See Fig. d). Now sew
both edges marked 2 together in the
same way and continue around the
edges until sides 7 have been
seamed. Turn bag right side out, fill
with beans or whatever and
ladderstitch sides of 8 together.

BALL GAMES

In the nursery, balls are very important toys as they help youngsters develop so many different skills. The Space Ball is rather futuristic in style, spinning like a flying saucer when thrown as well as producing sound. The Football on the other hand is more traditional and play with it will eventually introduce youngsters to the social skills needed for team games with rules, winning and losing.

MATERIALS NEEDED FOR FOOTBALL

46 cm (18 in) square of white velour fur
30.5 cm (12 in) square of black velour fur
224 g (8 oz) stuffing

Circumference of Football 56 cm (22 in)

MATERIALS NEEDED FOR SPACE BALL

Remnants of three different coloured cotton prints
56 g (2 oz) stuffing
Cylindrical chime approximately 6 cm (2½ in) tall

Circumference of Space Ball 36cm (14 in)

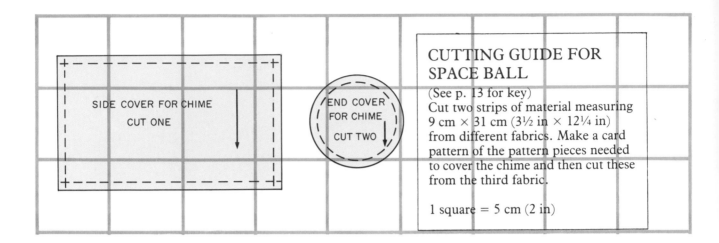

SIDE COVER FOR CHIME

CUT ONE

END COVER
FOR CHIME

CUT TWO

CUTTING GUIDE FOR SPACE BALL

(See p. 13 for key)
Cut two strips of material measuring 9 cm × 31 cm (3½ in × 12¼ in) from different fabrics. Make a card pattern of the pattern pieces needed to cover the chime and then cut these from the third fabric.

1 square = 5 cm (2 in)

MAKING THE SPACE BALL

1 Fold a strip lengthwise and with right sides together, seam one end and the long edge. Turn right side out and stuff. Join both ends together, making a ring. Prepare the second strip in the same way but before joining the ends together pass them through the first ring rather like a figure of eight. Now sew the ends together. (See Fig. a).

2 Seam the side cover for the chime, turn right side out and put over chime. Run a gathering thread around each end, pull up and fasten off. Turn under edge of top cover and sew in place inserting a little stuffing to mask the gathers. Cover bottom of chime in the same way. (See Fig. b). Push the chime between the strips so that it lies centrally with the strips forming a double coiled collar. Hold the chime in place by stitching to the collar.

a

b

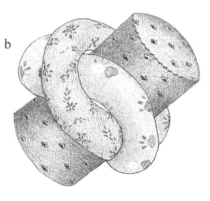

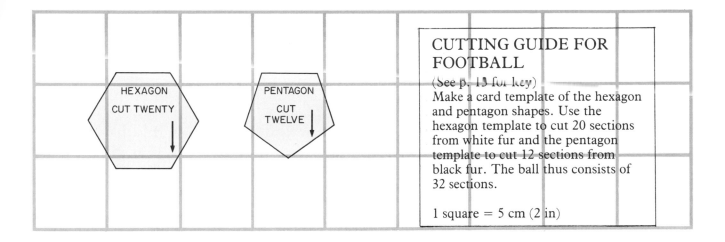

HEXAGON

CUT TWENTY ↓

PENTAGON

CUT TWELVE ↓

CUTTING GUIDE FOR FOOTBALL

(See p. 13 for key)

Make a card template of the hexagon and pentagon shapes. Use the hexagon template to cut 20 sections from white fur and the pentagon template to cut 12 sections from black fur. The ball thus consists of 32 sections.

1 square = 5 cm (2 in)

MAKING THE FOOTBALL

1 This ball is constructed by sewing each half in turn and then joining them together around the middle in a zig-zag seam. Start with a black pentagon and handsew by backstitching one edge of a white hexagon to each of its five sides. Sew adjacent sides of hexagons together so that the pentagon sits in a rosette. This completes the first round.

2 Make the second round by sewing the point of a pentagon between two hexagons. Five pentagons in all will be needed to complete the round. (See Fig. a). At this stage the ball begins to take shape, no longer will it lie flat.

3 Now sew a hexagon between each pentagon. The hexagon will be seamed on three sides leaving the other three sides free to fit into the other half of the ball. This third round completes half a ball. Make the other half in the same way.

4 Turn one half of the ball right side out and sit it inside the other half so that right sides are together. Align the edges by pinning a pentagon from one half to the protruding edge of a hexagon from the other half. (See Fig. b). When happy that all the pentagons are in place you can start to back stitch the halves together. Leave a stretch open for turning right side out. Stuff the ball moulding a firm, round shape. Close the opening with ladder stitch.

a

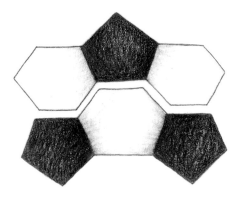

b

BABY BLACKFACE

Lambs are amongst the baby animals which are frequently found in the nursery as soft toys. This little Scottish blackface makes a change from the more traditional spring lambs with their pink ear linings and whiter-than-white coats.

MATERIALS NEEDED

46 cm (18 in) square of cream curl
    pile fur
30.5 cm (12 in) square of unpolished
    black fur
78 g (3 oz) stuffing
A pair of 12 mm brown safety eyes
Embroidery thread for nose

Length of Lamb 25.5 cm (10 in)

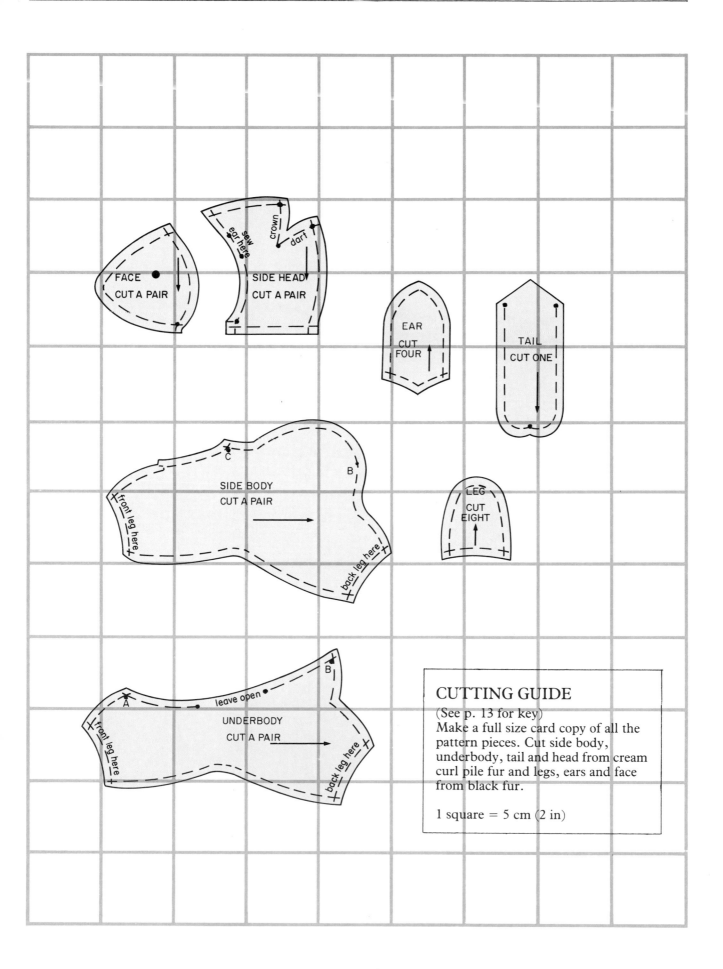

FACE
CUT A PAIR

crown
sew
ear here
dart
SIDE HEAD
CUT A PAIR

EAR
CUT
FOUR

TAIL
CUT ONE

C
B
SIDE BODY
CUT A PAIR
front leg here
back leg here

LEG
CUT
EIGHT

B
leave open
A
front leg here
UNDERBODY
CUT A PAIR
back leg here

CUTTING GUIDE

(See p. 13 for key)
Make a full size card copy of all the
pattern pieces. Cut side body,
underbody, tail and head from cream
curl pile fur and legs, ears and face
from black fur.

1 square = 5 cm (2 in)

MAKING THE BODY

1 Sew front legs, then back legs to both underbody pieces. Place underbodies right sides together and sew from A to B, leaving centre between match points open.

2 Sew front and back legs to both side bodies then, working on one side at a time, match to underbody and sew from A round legs to B. (See Fig. a). Bring side bodies together and sew from C back to B. Trim and clip seams as necessary. Put body aside for the moment.

MAKING THE HEAD

3 Make each side of the head in the following way. Sew ears together in pairs, turn right side out and fold open edges together. Tack to side head. (See Fig. b). Sew crown dart on top of side head.

4 Match face to side head and pin sides and centre to ensure a good fit. Sew. (See Fig. c). Place both completed heads together and sew from neck edge at front round head to neck edge at back.

5 Turn head right side out and fix eyes in place. Push head through neck opening of body, taking care to line up the seams of the head with the body seams. Oversew edges of neck together then backstitch by hand to make more secure. (See Fig. d).

6 Turn completed skin right side out through underbody opening. Stuff head firmly and body less so. Close opening with ladder stitch.

MAKING THE TAIL

7 Fold tail in half lengthways and sew long edges together. Turn right side out, position against rump and sew to the body.

8 Embroider nose and mouth with three strands of embroidery thread, finishing thread off invisibly by backstitching away around the neck seam. Carefully work over seams of legs and ears in particular to release any trapped fur.

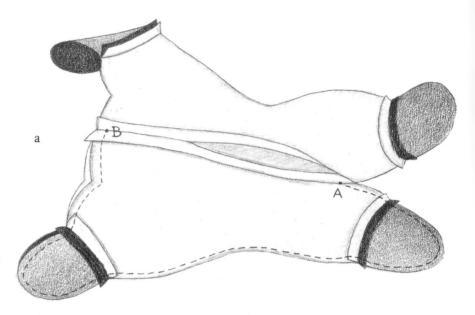

a

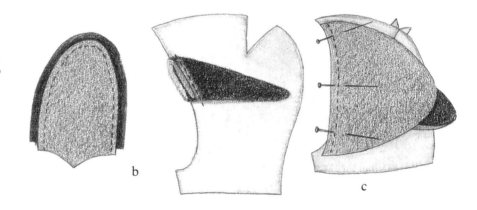

b

c

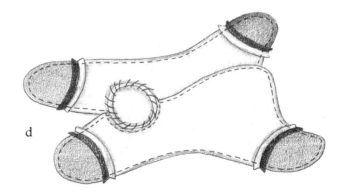

d

PERCIVAL TROTTER

*Here is a rather lovable pig that is little more than a bundle
of fluff to snuggle up to. He relies entirely on deep pile fur
for his skin and large doleful eyes with droopy eyelids to
provide his own special charm.*

MATERIALS NEEDED

61 cm (24 in) square of pink fur with
   a pile depth of 25 mm (1 in)
30.5 cm (12 in) square of pink velour
280 g (10 oz) stuffing
15 cm (6 in) narrow elastic
Brown embroidery thread
A pair of 22 mm brown safety eyes

Length of Pig 29 cm (11½ in)

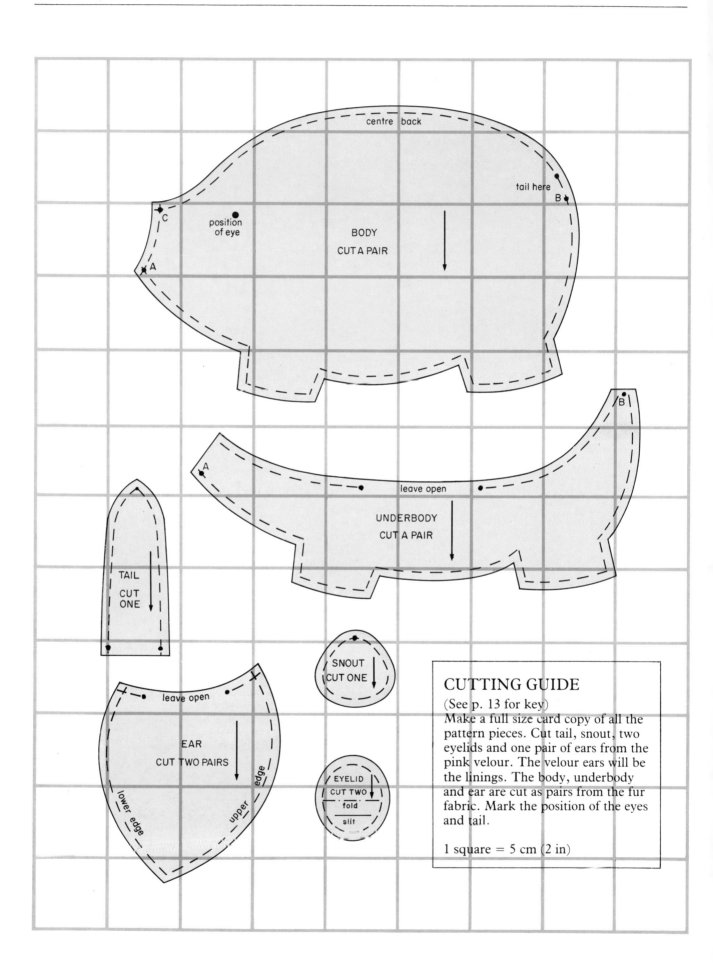

centre back

tail here

B

C

position
of eye

A

BODY
CUT A PAIR

B

A

leave open

UNDERBODY
CUT A PAIR

TAIL

CUT
ONE

leave open

EAR

CUT TWO PAIRS

lower edge

upper edge

SNOUT
CUT ONE

EYELID

CUT TWO

fold

slit

CUTTING GUIDE

(See p. 13 for key)

Make a full size card copy of all the
pattern pieces. Cut tail, snout, two
eyelids and one pair of ears from the
pink velour. The velour ears will be
the linings. The body, underbody
and ear are cut as pairs from the fur
fabric. Mark the position of the eyes
and tail.

1 square = 5 cm (2 in)

MAKING THE TAIL

1 Fold tail in half lengthways and sew curved edges together. Stitch the length of elastic across the tip of the tail. Turn tail right side out and pull on the elastic until the tail curls up to a pleasing shape. Sew across the open end of the tail, fastening the elastic at the same time. (See Fig. a). With raw edges level and right sides together sew the tail to a body piece.

MAKING THE BODY

2 Sew underbodies together leaving central section between match points open. (See Fig. b).

3 Open underbody out flat and place one half against matching sidebody. Sew back from snout at A round both legs to base of tail at B. (See Fig. c). Repeat on other side.

4 Refold skin to sew centre back seam of body from snout at C to B. (The last section of this seam is probably easier to sew by hand

because of the bulk of the tail and underbody.) Clip corners at top of legs and turn skin right side out. Check position of eyes and fix in place. (See Fig. d).

5 Turn skin wrong side out and sew snout in place. Position a ball of stuffing against the snout and hold in place with long stitches worked across the snout from seams at either side. Turn right side out and stuff the body. Close underbody opening with ladder stitch. (See Fig. e).

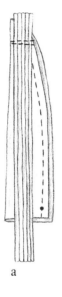

a

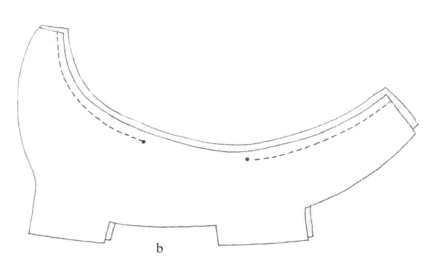

b

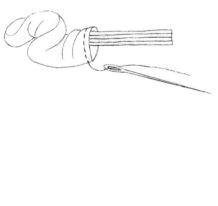

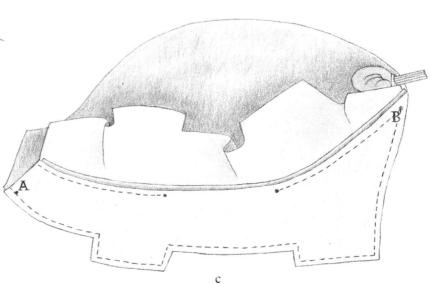

c

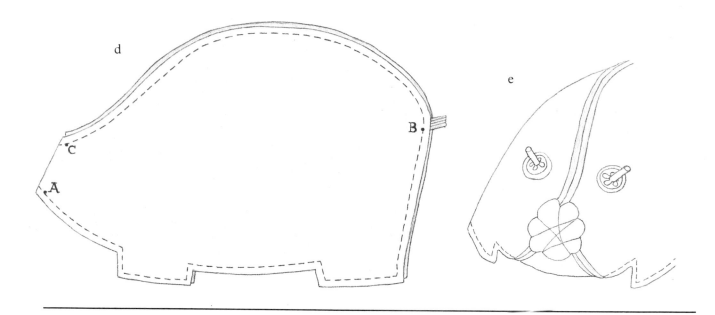

MAKING EYES AND TROTTERS

6 Fold eyelid in half and sew curved edges together. Trim seam and turn right side out through the slit. Insert a little stuffing into the eyelid to give it some shape. Close opening with cross stitch then place eyelid over eye and sew in place. Make second eyelid in the same way. Work two blocks of brown straight stitches on the snout for the nostrils.

7 The front legs are shorter than the hind legs and are liable to collapse if not strengthened. This can be achieved by taking a stitch from the front leg seam down to the bottom seam and out at the front again. Pull up to draw the seams together and work a few more stitches on top of the first to secure. Make sure that there is stuffing trapped within the stitch. This effectively makes a trotter of the front leg. Work opposite front leg in the same way.

MAKING THE EARS

8 Place an ear and velour ear lining together and sew round upper and lower edges. Trim seams and turn ear right side out. Turn in raw edges and oversew together pulling up slightly to curl the base of the ear. Make second ear in the same way and check at this stage that you have made a pair.

9 Place ears at an angle on the body and move them around until you are happy with the position. Pin the corners down to hold them in place and, with the ears laid back,

ladderstitch the front to the body first then turn the ears forward and stitch the back to the body. (See Fig. f). This order of sewing will hold the ears forward.

FINISHING OFF

10 Percival Trotter is now finished and only requires careful trimming of the long fur. Remove some fur from around the eyes and snout to reduce the bulk. Brush all seams to free any trapped pile.

f

SWEET DREAMS

The Man in the Moon is a doll with a difference for Brahms' Lullaby is tucked away inside him just waiting to be heard. This toy also provides additional enjoyment for a wide-awake youngster when hung as a mobile over his cot.

MATERIALS NEEDED

46 cm (18 in) square of yellow fur

7.5 cm (3 in) square of red felt

30.5 cm (12 in) square of brushed cotton for cap

23 cm × 92 cm (9 in × 36 in) wide fabric for limbs

220 g (8 oz) stuffing

A musical unit with a pull cord

Brown, black, blue and red embroidery threads

1m (1 yard) strong ribbon or tape for hanging loop, pompom or tassel to decorate cap

Height of Doll 37 cm (14½ in)

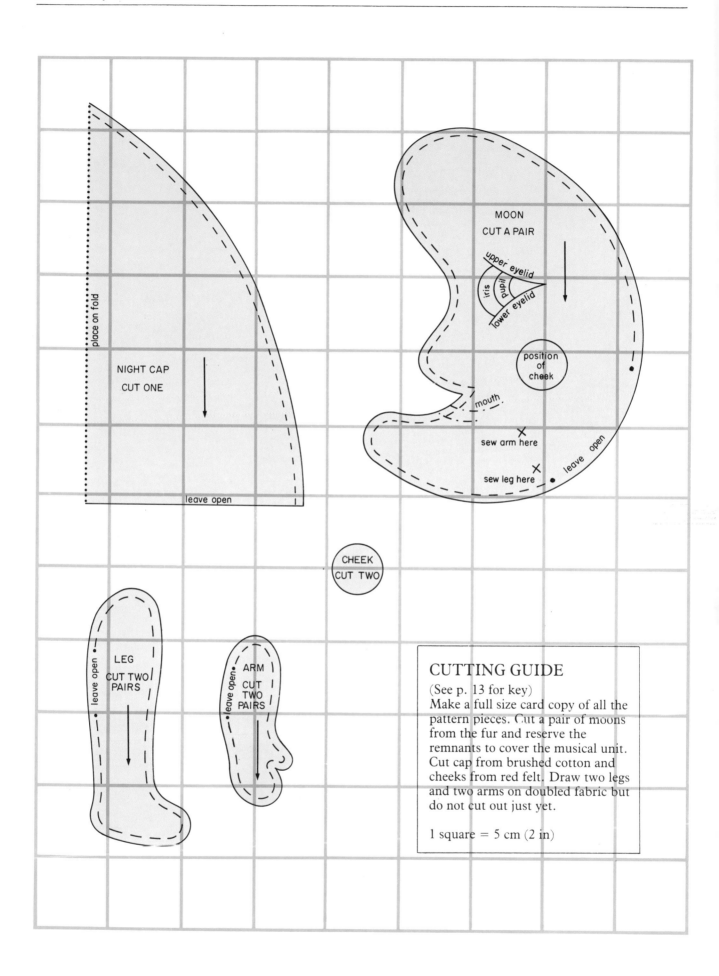

place on fold

NIGHT CAP
CUT ONE

leave open

MOON
CUT A PAIR

upper eyelid
iris
pupil
lower eyelid

position
of
cheek

mouth

sew arm here ✕

sew leg here ✕

leave open

CHEEK
CUT TWO

LEG
CUT TWO
PAIRS

leave open

ARM
CUT
TWO
PAIRS

leave open

CUTTING GUIDE
(See p. 13 for key)
Make a full size card copy of all the pattern pieces. Cut a pair of moons from the fur and reserve the remnants to cover the musical unit. Cut cap from brushed cotton and cheeks from red felt. Draw two legs and two arms on doubled fabric but do not cut out just yet.

1 square = 5 cm (2 in)

MAKING THE BODY

1 Topstitch by machine or simply hem cheeks to each moon. Stemstitch upper and lower eyelids with three strands of dark brown embroidery thread. Fill in pupil with black satin stitches. Again use three strands of embroidery thread and if necessary work the outline of each area with stem stitch as a guide before filling in with satin stitch. (See Fig. a). Sew heads together leaving open between match points. Clip corner at base of nose and turn moon right side out. (See Fig. b).

2 Wrap music box in fabric, taking care not to trap the pull cord. Stitch the cover in place to hold securely. Stuff top of moon, nose and chin then insert the covered musical unit with the pull cord lying against the opening. Stuff around the unit and close the opening with ladder stitch. (See Fig. c).

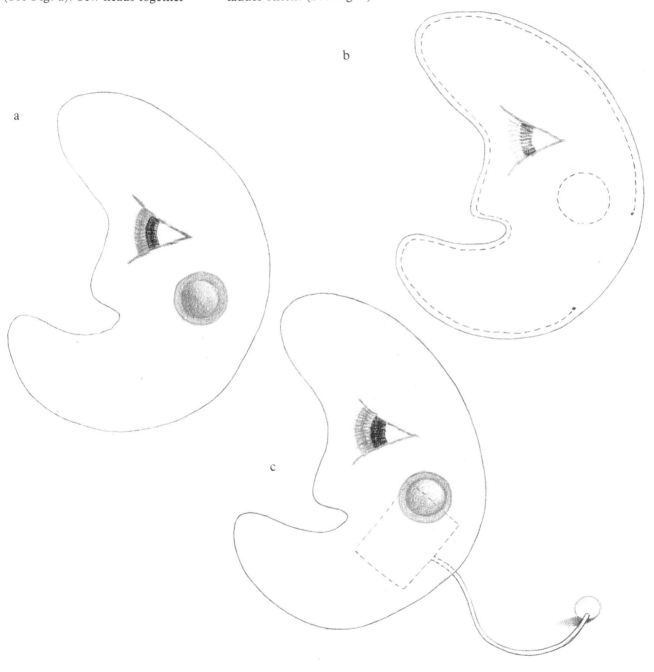

MAKING THE MOUTH AND LIMBS

3 Stemstitch mouth with three strands of red embroidery thread. Then pin corners of limb fabric to hold the double layer together. Sew arms and legs 6 mm (¼ in) inside the pencil line, leaving open between match points. Now cut each limb out on the pencil line and turn right side out. Take care with the thumbs.

4 Stuff each limb and close opening with ladder stitch. Position limbs against Xs marked on each side of the moon and sew in place. (See Fig. d). Fold hanging tape in half to make a loop and sew the ends across the back seam of the moon. The tapes must be secure to hold the weight of the toy.

MAKING THE NIGHT CAP

5 Make night cap by folding in half and sewing the curved back seam. Turn right side out and press lower edge to the inside. Place cap on head and hem in place. (See Fig. e).

FINISHING OFF

6 Pull hanging loop upwards over edge of cap and stitch down approximately 2.5 cm (1 in) beyond edge. The exact position will determine the angle that the Man in the Moon hangs from. Trim cap with a pompom or tassel sewn to the top then fold cap over to a pleasing position and hold in place with a catch stitch.

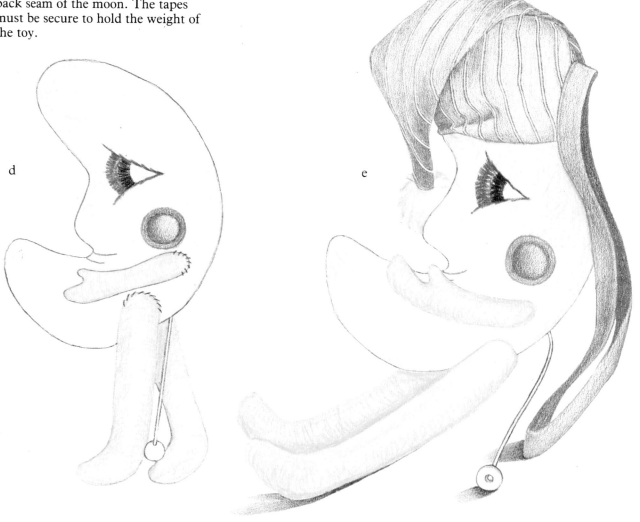

d

e

DOLLS

There can hardly be a child anywhere that hasn't had a doll of some sort to play with during early childhood. Such dolls have been fashioned throughout time from a wide variety of materials from plaited straw to whittled wood, bound fibres to cut paper, skins, wool fibres and woven textiles. Rag dolls are the softest and most cuddly of all the dolls that children will play with and are more likely to be homemade with individual loving care rather than mass-produced in a factory like their modern day vinyl sisters.

The Gingham Girls are truly simple, a few remnants and a little time being all that is required to start you on your way. The clowns introduce both the problems and joys of working with stretch fabrics and this is taken further when used to make the softly sculptured Baby Love. She has the additional attraction of her very own carry cot and mini Teddy and will prove invaluable to youngsters who want a little one of their own to look after. A touch of history is embodied in the fighting men while the collection concludes with the international children who come from all corners of the globe.

1. Gingham Girls
2. Loose Tubes
3. Pierrot
4. Able Seaman Ben
5. Yeoman Warder Hal
6. Baby Love
7. Baby Love's Carry Cot and Teddy
8. Global Children

GINGHAM GIRLS

Rag dolls have traditionally been made from readily available remnants and these dolls, with their fun coloured gingham bodies, are no exception. By simply ringing the changes with two basic yarn hairstyles and altering the dress trims you can quickly make a different lass for each day of the week.

MATERIALS NEEDED FOR ONE DOLL

30.5 cm × 92 cm (12 in × 36 in) wide small check gingham
170 g (6 oz) stuffing
11 m (12 yards) mohair yarn for hair
30.5 cm × 92 cm (12 in × 36 in) wide cotton print

A small piece of felt for eyes
53 cm (21 in) bias binding to neaten neck
Additional lace to trim dress as required
23 cm (9 in) narrow elastic

Height of each Doll 30.5 cm (12 in)

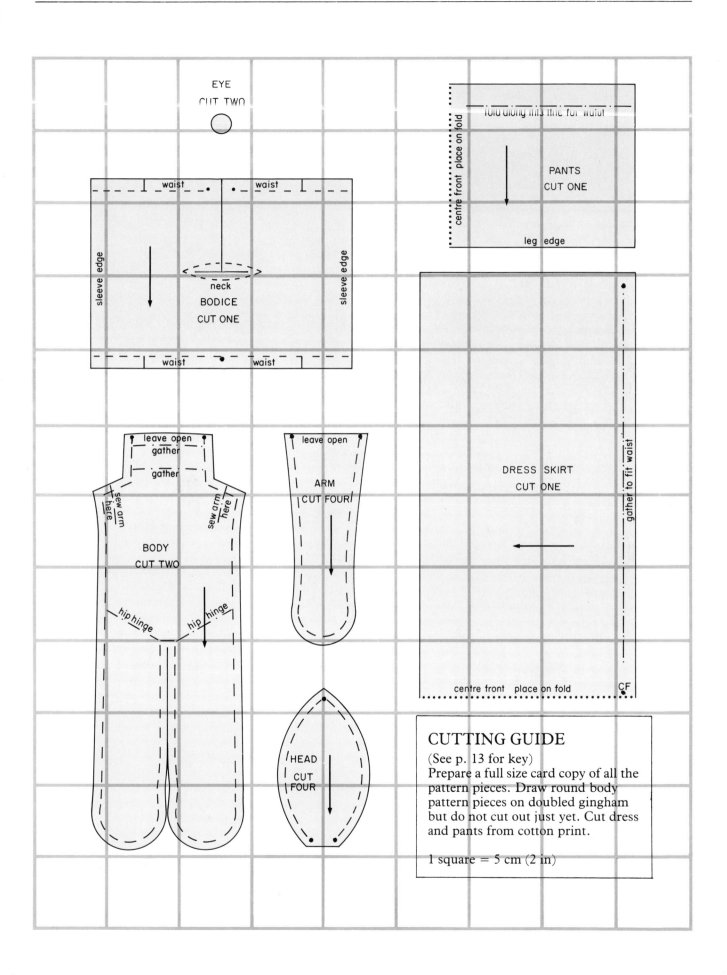

CUTTING GUIDE

(See p. 13 for key)
Prepare a full size card copy of all the
pattern pieces. Draw round body
pattern pieces on doubled gingham
but do not cut out just yet. Cut dress
and pants from cotton print.

1 square = 5 cm (2 in)

MAKING THE BODY

1 Sew body and both arms through the doubled fabric with a narrow seam. Leave the top straight edges open. Sew each pair of head pieces down one curved side only. Cut out all the pieces, clipping into corners at the top of the legs. Turn body and arms right side out.

2 Sew paired head sections together on remaining curved sides then turn head right side out. Stuff firmly, being careful to retain a rounded shape. Stuff legs firmly up to the top then pin across each leg at an angle sloping to the outside. Work a neat stab stitch across the angle to make hip hinges. Stuff remainder of the body very firmly.

3 Gather top of neck to hold stuffing in place. Work a second row of gathering 12 mm (½ in) below the edge. This results in a firm neck stalk. Twist head down on to neck and ladderstitch in place with seams at side of face rather than centre front.

4 Stuff each arm nearly to the top and pin to hold stuffing away from the opening. Turn in raw edges making a small pleat on each side to reduce the width. Oversew sides together. (See Fig. a). Lay an arm on each shoulder and sew securely in place.

5 Cut two small circles of felt for the eyes and attach them to the face with straight stitches caught down in the middle. The mouth could also be a straight stitch pulled down in the centre to form a V. The presence of a mouth will depend on the size and colour of the check gingham.

MAKING THE HAIR

6 To make plaits, start by cutting the yarn into fifty-eight 38 cm (15 in) lengths. Divide into two equal-sized bundles. Take one bundle and lay it centrally across the back of the head and backstitch in place over each ear position in turn.

7 Lay remaining bundle across front and top of head, spreading the strands for a good cover. Again, backstitch in place on each side. Finish by plaiting the long ends and trimming. (See Fig. b). Bunches are a variation of the plaited hairstyle. Use less wool and cut forty-eight 20 cm (8 in) lengths. Divide into two bundles and attach to the head in exactly the same way as the plaits. Trim ends neatly.

8 Curls are made by winding yarn over a 12 mm knitting needle and stemstitching the loops together along the length. You will need approximately three needle-loads to make sufficient curls. Position curls on the head and backstitch in place. (See Fig. c).

a

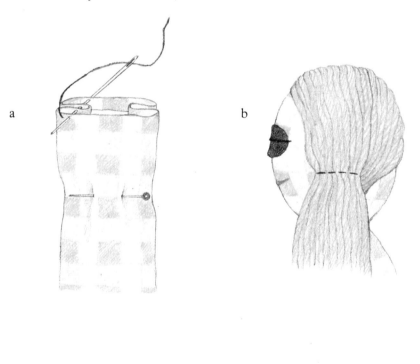

b

c

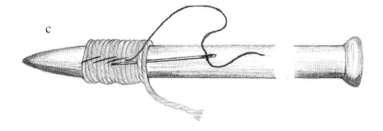

MAKING THE CLOTHES

9 Fold pants right side together and sew short edges together. Make a narrow hem along one long edge. This will be the leg edge. Make a wider hem along the remaining edge for the waist, leaving a small opening. Topstitch the fold so that a casing is formed. Thread elastic through the casing and pull up to fit the doll. Fasten ends of elastic together and close the opening.

10 Turn pants right side out and press flat with seam at centre back. Topstitch through both layers at the lower edge for a short distance. This results in two leg openings on a very simple garment.

11 Make a narrow hem on both sleeve edges. Fold bodice and sew short underarm seams. Clip into seam allowance at the inside edge of the seam to free the sleeves from the waist edge. Gather waist edge of skirt and pull up to fit the bodice. Sew skirt to bodice, being careful to fold sleeves out of the way. (See Fig. d). Neaten both back edges of the dress and the lower edge of the skirt by sewing a narrow hem on all three sides.

12 Fit dress on doll to check the fit of the neck opening. Make any necessary adjustments. Centre the bias binding on the neck and sew in place. Trim neck. (See Fig. e). Fold bias binding to wrong side of neck and topstitch the two edges together. Knot each end of the ties.

13 Finish dress by overlapping back edges of skirt and top stitching them together from below the waist to the hem. You may need a snap or hook and eye at the waist edge.

d
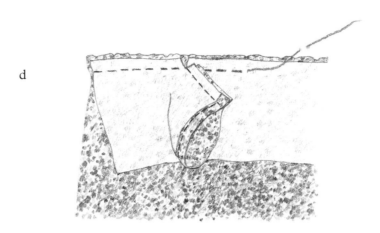

e
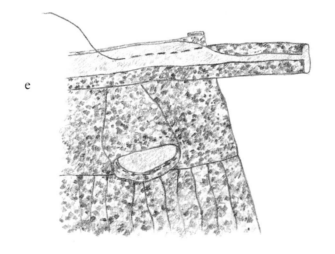

LOOSE TUBES

This little chap, with his deceptively simple costumed body, is a sure winner with toymakers. There is no conventional body as such, only hands, feet and head. All the rest is loosely filled tubes which are fitted together and then dressed with a smock which itself is another tube. A crown of colourful curls finishes off the clown.

MATERIALS NEEDED

46 cm × 115 cm (18 in × 45 in) wide cotton print

170 g (6 oz) stuffing

18 cm (7 in) square of black felt

3.5 cm (1¼ in) diameter flat button

A small piece of red felt or brushed cotton for nose

A packet of 12 mm (½ in) bias binding

25 cm (10 in) square of flesh-coloured stockinette

25 cm (10 in) square of stretch interfacing

A ball of double knit yarn for hair

Red lipstick or blush powder

Height of Doll 35 cm (14 in)

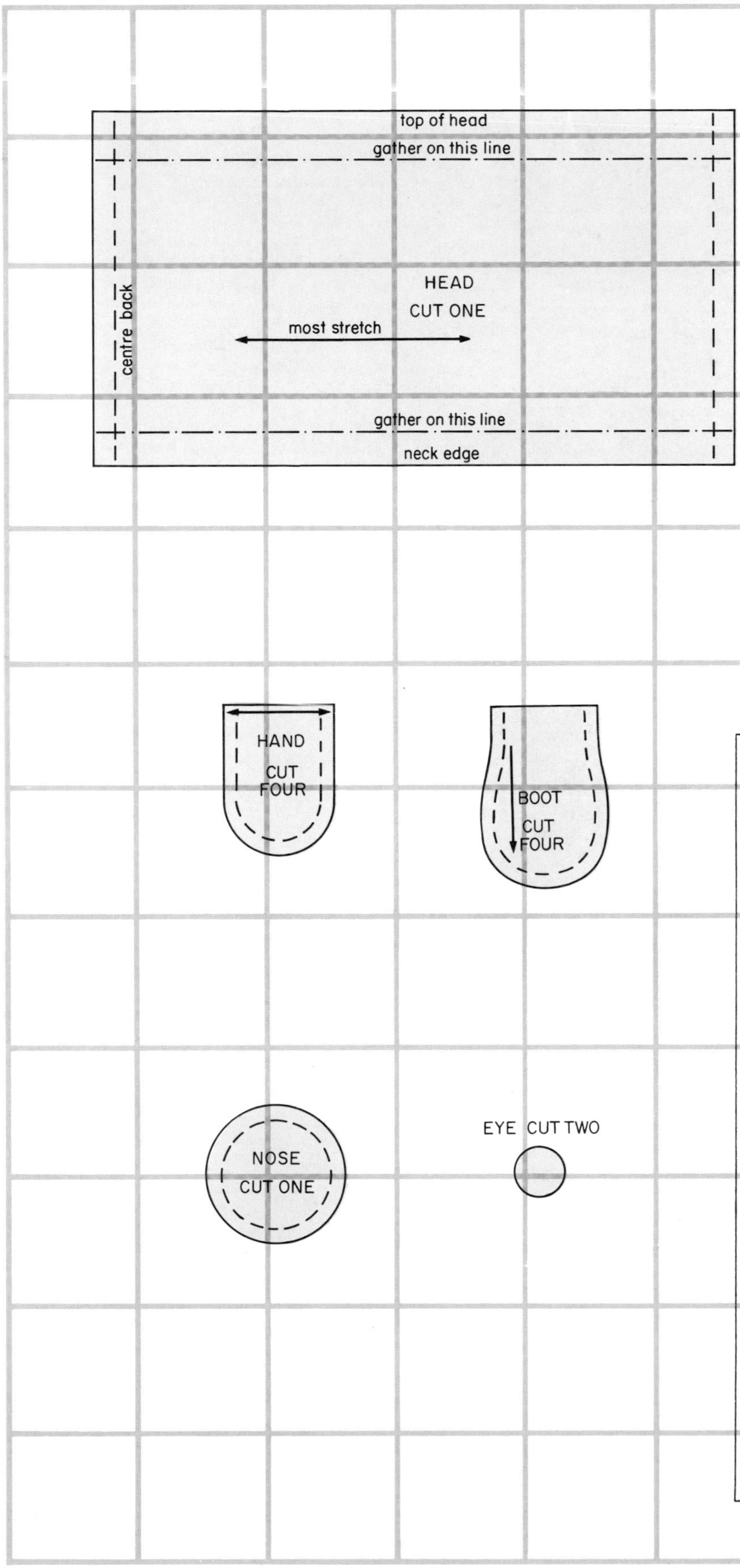

top of head
gather on this line

centre back

HEAD
CUT ONE

most stretch

gather on this line
neck edge

HAND
CUT
FOUR

BOOT
CUT
FOUR

NOSE
CUT ONE

EYE CUT TWO

CUTTING GUIDE

(See p. 13 for key)
Prepare a full size card copy of all the
pattern pieces. In addition you will
need to make paper patterns for the
clothes as follows:-

Trouser legs 20 cm × 56 cm
            (8 in × 22 in)
Sleeve   20 cm × 18 cm
            (8 in × 7 in)
Smock   25 cm × 56 cm
            (10 in × 22 in)

Cut one trouser leg, two sleeves
and one smock from the cotton
print. Cut boots and eyes from black
felt and nose from the red fabric. Cut
head and hands from stockinette that
has been backed with the stretch
interfacing. (Without this
preparation this stockinette would
stretch too much on stuffing and
distort.) Remember to cut pieces
with most stretch going around the
head and hands.

1 square = 5 cm (2 in)

MAKING THE BODY

1 Sew two boot pieces together with a narrow seam round the curved edge. Turn right side out and stuff very firmly. Run a gathering thread around the open edge and pull up slightly to draw edges inwards. Work a few straight stitches across the opening to hold the stuffing in place. Make a second boot in the same way and set aside. (See Fig. a).

2 Neaten both short edges of the trouser legs with bias binding first then sew long edges together to make a tube. Turn right side out. The bias binding makes a brightly coloured edging.

3 Fold trouser tube in half with seam lying centrally on inside. Tie centre fold with strong thread and finish by using same thread to sew button on top of the fold. Stuff each half of the tube loosely and not quite to the bottom edges. Run a gathering thread round each ankle, about 2.5 cm (1 in) behind the edge. Insert ankle of boot into trouser leg and pull up gathers. Attach boot and leg by backstitching through the gathers. (See Fig. b). Attach remaining boot in the same way.

4 Sew short sides of head together and turn right side out. Run a strong gathering thread along the neck edge and start to pull up. Insert neck button through gathers to lodge inside head then pull up tight and fasten off with seam at back. Distribute fullness evenly round neck. Stuff head carefully, retaining a good rounded shape. Gather crown edge and pull up turning raw edges inwards. Fasten off. The neck can be made more securely by ladder-stitching the head to the trouser legs beyond the edge of the button.

a

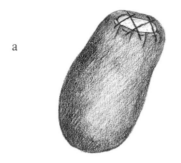

b

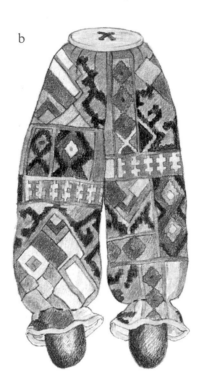

MAKING THE SMOCK

5 Join short sides of smock together with a french seam and neaten bottom edge with bias binding. Fold top edge to inside by 5.5 cm (2¼ in) and press to make a crisp edge. Topstitch bias binding to the folded edge.

6 Run a gathering thread through the doubled top layer approximately 4 cm (1½ in) back from the edge. Dress smock on body and pull up to fit round the neck. Sew through gathers to body beneath. The top fold becomes the ruff and the seam should lie at the centre back. (See Fig. c).

7 Take a pair of hand pieces and sew them together round the curved edge. Turn right side out and stuff firmly taking care not to lose the shape. Finish wrist edge in the same way as described for the ankles of the boots. Make second hand.

8 Neaten one long edge of each sleeve with bias binding. This is the wrist. Fold each sleeve in turn and sew short edges together, turn right side out. Gather sleeve behind the wrist, insert hand and finish pulling up gathers to fit tightly against the hand. Sew hand and sleeve together through the gathers. Stuff sleeve tube loosely, turn in raw edges at top and over sew sleeve in place on the shoulder. Finish other sleeve in the same way and sew on to the smock.

c

FINISHING THE HEAD

9 Turn under raw edge of nose fabric and gather. Stuff firmly then pull up tight on gathering thread to make a ball nose. Ladderstitch centrally to the face. Build up colour on cheeks by smearing on lipstick with your little finger. Alternatively, use blush powder.

10 Position eyes and hold each in place with an upright cross stitch caught down in the middle. Use ordinary black sewing thread rather than embroidery silks and extend stitches at side and bottom beyond the felt circle. The thread can start behind the eye and finish off under the hairline, out of sight. (See Fig. d).

11 Make a hair frame by cutting a strong piece of card measuring 34 cm × 5 cm (13½ in × 2 in). Cut a central slot from the card along the long axis leaving a bridge at each end of approximately 2 cm (¾ in) wide.

12 Wind yarn evenly along length of frame. Backstitch or machine strands together through the slot. Cut loops to remove fringe from frame. (See Fig. e). Prepare a second fringe in the same way.

13 If you prefer your clown to have curls then you will have to break the bridge at one end of the frame and slide the hair off. This means making a new frame to wind the second lot of curls. Arrange curls on head so that they frame the face and backstitch in place through the fringe stitching. Two lengths of curls should be sufficient to cover the head but if you find that it is sparse, simply wind and prepare another length.

d

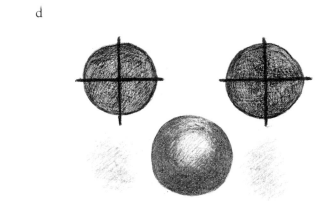

e

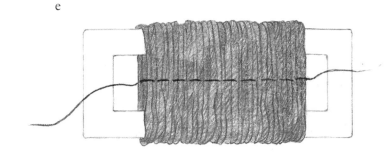

PIERROT

*Pierrot, with his familiar white costume and whitened face,
is a popular character from the Italian Commedia dell'arte.
He is the sad-faced clown, unsuccessful in love.
Why not make him happy by using the same pattern to
make his beloved Columbine? All that is needed is a longer
smock and a girlish face.*

MATERIALS NEEDED

60 cm × 115 cm (24 in × 45 in) wide
  white satin
15 cm × 92 cm (6 in × 36 in) wide
  black satin
23 cm × 142 cm (9 in × 56 in) wide
  white stockinette
A small piece of flesh-coloured
  stockinette for nose
170 g (6 oz) stuffing
A flat button, 3.5 cm (1¼ in) in
  diameter
56 cm (22 in) of 6 mm (¼ in) black
  satin ribbon
3 small black pompoms
Black felt for eyes
Silver metallic thread
23 cm (9 in) any width of stretch
  interfacing
blush powder or red lipstick

Height of Doll 35 cm (14 in)

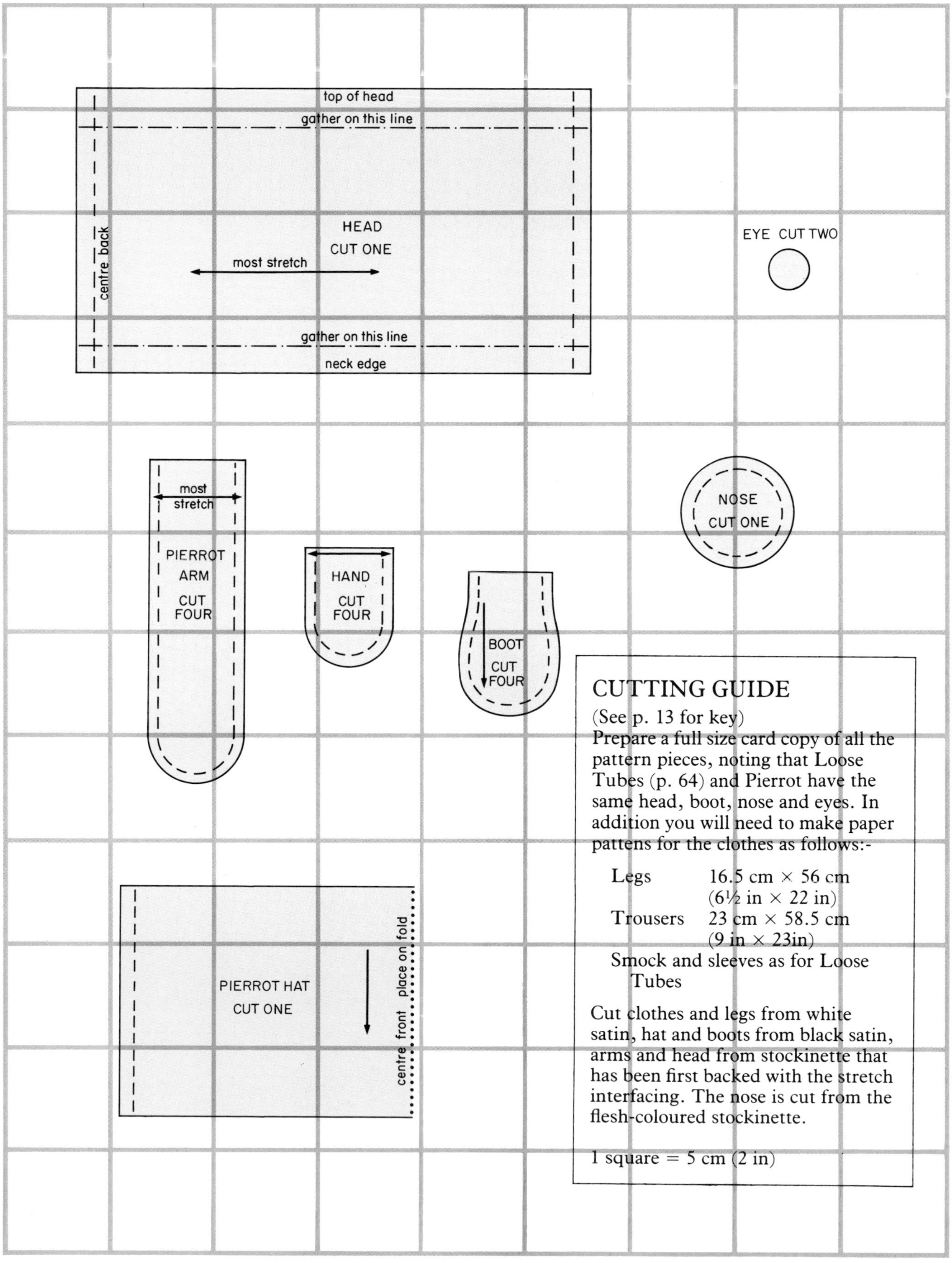

top of head

gather on this line

centre back

HEAD

CUT ONE

most stretch

gather on this line

neck edge

EYE CUT TWO

most
stretch

PIERROT
ARM
CUT
FOUR

HAND
CUT
FOUR

NOSE
CUT ONE

BOOT
CUT
FOUR

PIERROT HAT
CUT ONE

centre front place on fold

CUTTING GUIDE
(See p. 13 for key)

Prepare a full size card copy of all the pattern pieces, noting that Loose Tubes (p. 64) and Pierrot have the same head, boot, nose and eyes. In addition you will need to make paper pattens for the clothes as follows:-

Legs	16.5 cm × 56 cm
	(6½ in × 22 in)
Trousers	23 cm × 58.5 cm
	(9 in × 23in)

Smock and sleeves as for Loose Tubes

Cut clothes and legs from white satin, hat and boots from black satin, arms and head from stockinette that has been first backed with the stretch interfacing. The nose is cut from the flesh-coloured stockinette.

1 square = 5 cm (2 in)

MAKING THE BODY

1 Much of the making of Pierrot is similar to that of Loose Tubes (p. 64) so you should read and refer to both sets of directions. Make the boots as outlined for Loose Tubes. Sew the long edges of the legs together to make a tube. Fold in half, gather the fold and fasten off. Now lightly stuff each leg. Turn under raw ankle edges and gather each leg on to a boot.

2 Sew long edges of trousers together to make a tube. Hem both short edges. Now turn trousers right side out and feed over legs. Gather middle of trousers to legs beneath and then sew the button to the top side ready for the head. Make the head and attach to the button as outlined for Loose Tubes. Stuff and close off the top opening.

3 Sew short edges of the smock together with a french seam. Now turn top edge forward to inside by 5 cm (2 in) and sew the black ribbon against the edge. Make a narrow hem along the bottom edge. Turn smock right side out and dress on body by gathering to the neck as described for Loose Tubes. Decorate the front with a couple of pompoms.

4 Sew arm pieces together in pairs around the curved edges. Turn right side out and stuff. Tuck in raw edges and oversew edges together.

5 Hem one long edge of each sleeve. Fold sleeves in half and sew each in turn into a tube. Turn sleeves right side out and fill each with an arm. Turn under raw edge at the top and gather on to the arm. Sew an arm on each shoulder.

FINISHING THE HEAD

6 Make nose and eyes as outlined for Loose Tubes. Blush cheeks as for Loose Tubes (p. 64). Work a small upside-down fly stitch in black sewing thread for the mouth. (See Fig. a).

7 The single tear drop is achieved by embroidering a detached chain stitch just beneath one of the eyes. Work a smaller chain stitch inside the original stitch to give more depth.

8 Seam the short edges of the hat together. Gather one long edge and pull up tight with the raw edges on the wrong side. Now sew a pompom over the gathers on the right side. (See Fig. b). Turn under remaining long edge of the hat and place on the head. Check that the seam is at the centre back before sewing in place.

a

b

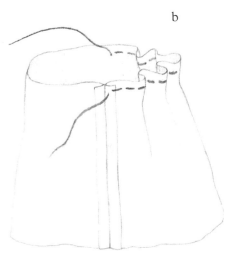

ABLE SEAMAN BEN

*Ben is wearing the centuries-old sailor costume of
bell-bottomed trousers and distinctive square collar. This
style was adopted by patriotic parents for their children
during the Victorian and Edwardian eras and it has
remained a firm favourite ever since, girls wearing pleated skirts
in place of the trousers. Ben's outfit is simplified and
sewn in with the body, making him an ideal mascot doll.*

MATERIALS NEEDED

15 cm × 92 cm (6 in × 36 in) wide
   calico
23 cm × 114 cm (9 in × 45 in) wide
   blue cotton
23 cm × 92 cm (9 in × 36 in) wide
   white cotton
15 cm × 46 cm (6 in × 18 in) black
   cotton
15 cm × 46 cm (6 in × 18 in)
   interfacing
140 g (5 oz) stuffing
6 m (6 yards) brown wool for hair
28 cm (11 in) of 1.5 cm (⅝ in) wide
   navy blue ribbon
59 cm (23 in) of 1 cm (⅜ in) wide
   navy blue ribbon
Brown embroidery thread
2 navy blue domed buttons for eyes
Blush powder

Height of Ben 30.5 cm (12 in)

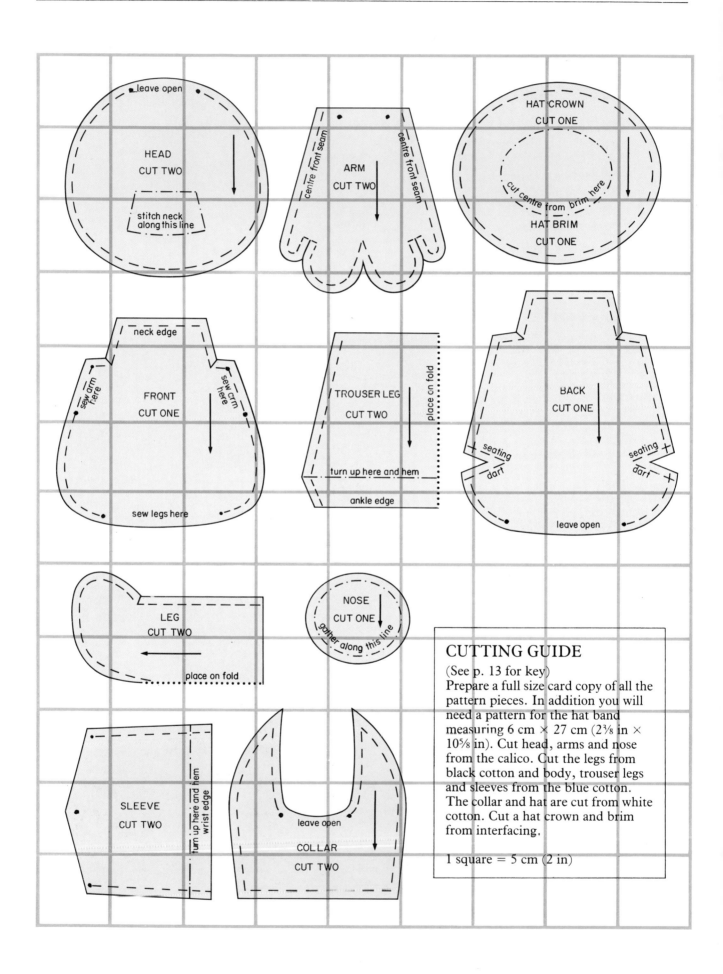

HEAD
CUT TWO
leave open
stitch neck along this line

ARM
CUT TWO
centre front seam
centre front seam

HAT CROWN
CUT ONE
cut centre from brim here
HAT BRIM
CUT ONE

FRONT
CUT ONE
neck edge
sew arm here
sew arm here
sew legs here

TROUSER LEG
CUT TWO
place on fold
turn up here and hem
ankle edge

BACK
CUT ONE
seating dart
seating dart
leave open

LEG
CUT TWO
place on fold

NOSE
CUT ONE
gather along this line

SLEEVE
CUT TWO
turn up here and hem
wrist edge

COLLAR
CUT TWO
leave open

CUTTING GUIDE

(See p. 13 for key)
Prepare a full size card copy of all the pattern pieces. In addition you will need a pattern for the hat band measuring 6 cm × 27 cm (2⅜ in × 10⅝ in). Cut head, arms and nose from the calico. Cut the legs from black cotton and body, trouser legs and sleeves from the blue cotton. The collar and hat are cut from white cotton. Cut a hat crown and brim from interfacing.

1 square = 5 cm (2 in)

MAKING THE BODY

1 Fold arm in half and sew curved edge. Clip between the thumb and first finger then turn right side out. Stuff lower half and hold stuffing in place with a pin. Bring seam to centre front and press straight edges together. Shape the top of the arm by cutting at an angle from the bottom up to the top. (See Fig. a). Make the second arm in the same way but cut the angle in the opposite direction so that you have a left and a right arm.

2 Hem the wrist edge of each sleeve in turn then sew the side seams and turn right side out. Feed an arm up a sleeve until all raw edges are level. Sew arms to front side of the body. The thumbs should be facing forward. Remove pins from arms at this stage. (See Fig. b).

3 Fold leg in half and sew, leaving top straight edge open. Turn leg right side out and stuff firmly, nearly to the top. Hold stuffing in place with a pin. Make second leg in the same way.

4 Hem ankle edges of each trouser leg. Fold trouser legs in half and sew side seams in turn. Turn right side out and feed a leg into each trouser until raw edges are level at the top. Seams lie on the outside edge of the trousers. Tack legs together across the top. Sew legs to body front with toes pointing towards the neck and all raw edges level. Be careful to match centres. (See Fig. c).

5 Make the two seating darts in the back then sew front and back together leaving bottom edge open. Turn body right side out and stuff. Ladderstitch opening behind the legs. Remove pins from legs.

a

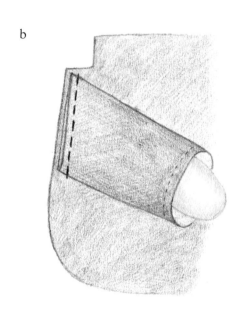

b

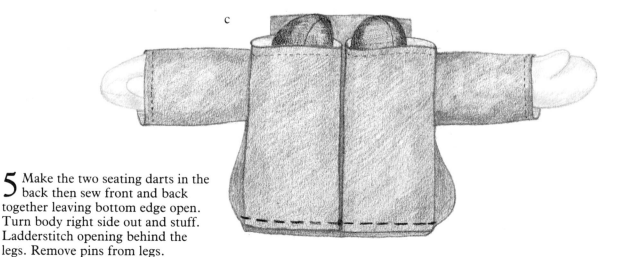

c

MAKING THE HEAD

6 Sew head pieces together round edge leaving the crown open. Trim seam then turn the head right side out and stuff firmly taking care to get a good, rounded shape. Close opening. Place the head against the neck and ladderstitch in position. Work across the top edge of the neck first then down each side and finally across the front of the neck. This will anchor the head more securely by pulling the chin in close to the body. (See Fig. d).

7 Turn under the edge of the nose and gather. Pull up, enclosing a ball of stuffing. Ladderstitch the nose to the centre of the face. Work around several times to make sure that it is securely held. Backstitch a strong doubled thread to the top of the head then use this to sew the eyes in place, pulling the eyes in tightly to sink them in sockets. Blush the cheeks and nose with face powder. Finish working the features by using three strands of embroidery thread to embroider a fly stitch mouth and eyebrows.

FINISHING OFF THE HEAD

8 The hairstyle for Ben is very simple. Wrap wool around a couple of fingers, thirteen times to make a small bundle. Make three more bundles in the same way. Machine all four bundles together close to one end to make a continuous strip. Don't worry about uneven lengths as these can be trimmed to size later. The loops at the machined edge will of course be hidden under the hat.

9 Lay strip on head so that hair starts on either side of the front and passes behind to cover the neck. Backstitch in place through the machine line. Cut loops at the bottom but do not trim just yet. Tack interfacing to the wrong side of the hat crown and likewise interfacing to the brim. Now place both hat pieces right sides together and sew round the edge. Trim seams and turn hat right side out. Make a small slit on one side of the brim.

10 Fold the hat band in half across the width. Lay the wide ribbon close to the folded edge and topstitch in place. Now sew the band to the brim with all raw edges level and starting at the slit in the brim. Turn hat wrong side out and fold bringing edges of slit together and the short ends of the band. Sew. Now turn hat right side out and put on the head. Catch in place on the sides. Trim the hair to the required length. (See Fig. e).

11 Sew the collar pieces together all round the edge leaving a small opening on the back neck edge. Trim seams and cut corners away. Turn collar right side out, close the opening then press. Now position the narrow ribbon on the collar and topstitch in place leaving the ends hanging at the front. Put collar around neck and catch in place to hold. Tie a bow in front and trim the ends to the required length. (See Fig. f).

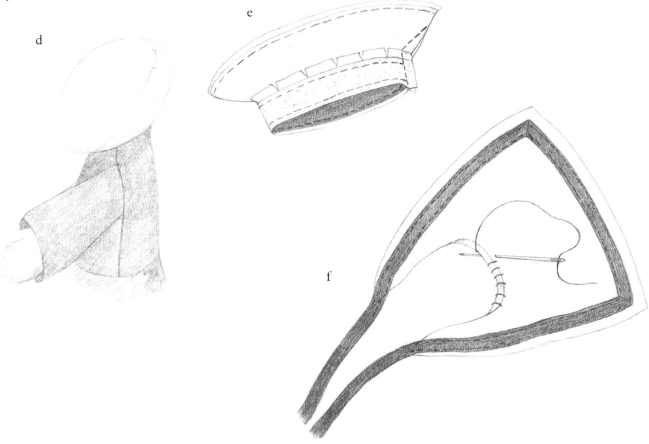

d

e

f

YEOMAN WARDER HAL

The colourful Tudor-costumed yeoman warders of the Tower of London are a popular attraction with the tourists and are known affectionately as the Beefeaters. They should not be confused with the Yeoman of the Guard who are similarly dressed.

MATERIALS NEEDED

15 cm × 92 cm (6 in × 36 in) wide calico

46 cm × 92 cm (18 in × 36 in) wide red brushed cotton

23 cm × 92 cm (9 in × 36 in) wide black cotton or fine wool

15 cm × 92 cm (6 in × 36 in) wide interfacing

140 g (5 oz) stuffing

7 m (7½ yards) white wool for hair

2 m (6 ft 6 in) gold braid or ribbon

Brown and old gold embroidery thread

2 navy blue domed buttons for eyes

Blush powder

63.5 cm (25 in) each of 1.5 cm (⅝ in) wide blue, red and white ribbon for hat rosettes

1.52 m (5 ft) of 25 mm (1 in) wide white grosgrain ribbon for ruff

24 cm (9½ in) narrow navy blue ribbon

28 cm (11 in) narrow white ribbon

32 cm (12½ in) of 1.5 cm (⅝ in) wide red ribbon

Height of Yeoman 30.5 cm (12 in)

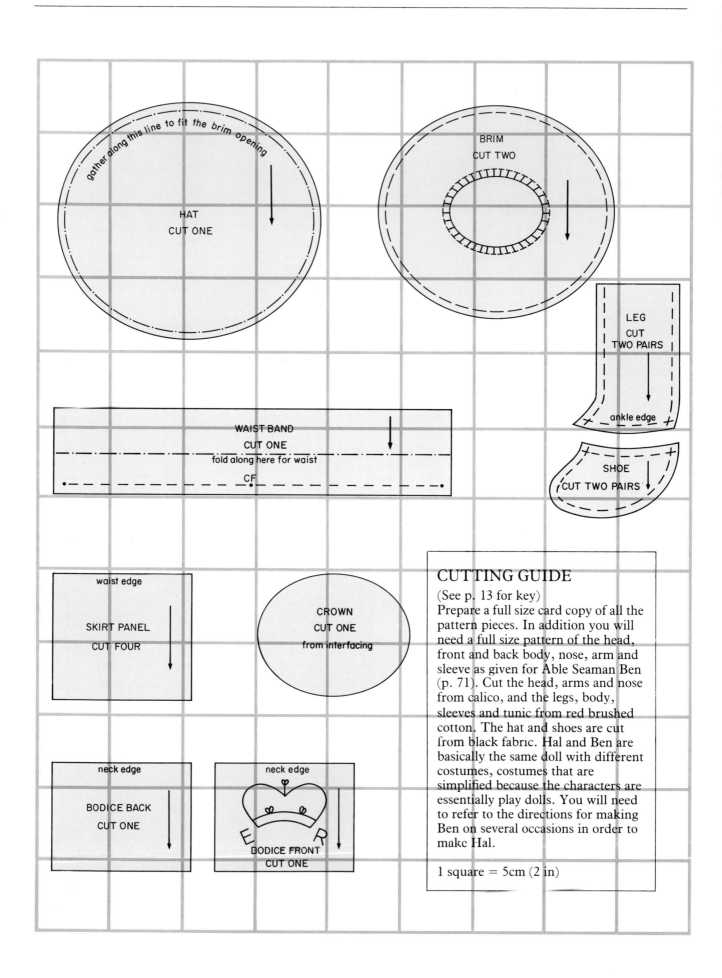

gather along this line to fit the brim opening

HAT
CUT ONE

BRIM
CUT TWO

LEG
CUT
TWO PAIRS

ankle edge

SHOE
CUT TWO PAIRS

WAIST BAND
CUT ONE
fold along here for waist
CF

waist edge

SKIRT PANEL
CUT FOUR

CROWN
CUT ONE
from interfacing

neck edge

BODICE BACK
CUT ONE

neck edge

E   R
BODICE FRONT
CUT ONE

CUTTING GUIDE
(See p. 13 for key)
Prepare a full size card copy of all the pattern pieces. In addition you will need a full size pattern of the head, front and back body, nose, arm and sleeve as given for Able Seaman Ben (p. 71). Cut the head, arms and nose from calico, and the legs, body, sleeves and tunic from red brushed cotton. The hat and shoes are cut from black fabric. Hal and Ben are basically the same doll with different costumes, costumes that are simplified because the characters are essentially play dolls. You will need to refer to the directions for making Ben on several occasions in order to make Hal.

1 square = 5cm (2 in)

MAKING THE BODY

1 Complete each leg section by sewing a shoe to the ankle then sew legs together in pairs leaving the tops open. Turn legs right side out and stuff very firmly nearly to the top. Press top edges together with seams lying centrally and then hold stuffing in place with a pin. Tack legs together side by side. Sew legs to front body with toes pointing towards the neck.

2 Make the arms as described for Ben (p. 71). Hem the wrist edge of the sleeves by turning the edge forward to the right side and covering with gold braid. Then sew side seams of sleeves, fit on arms and sew to the body. Finish making the body as outlined for Ben.

3 Neaten the neck edge of both bodice pieces by making a single hem. Now neaten all sides by turning edges forward and pressing to hold the fold. Lay bodice pieces right sides up with neck edges together in the centre. Starting on one side at the waist edge, topstitch braid over raw edge and continue across on to the second bodice piece. (See Fig. a). Cover the other side edges with braid in the same way. The braid forms the shoulders.

4 Work embroidered crown and initials on the bodice front. Stem stitch is used to outline the crown. Use three strands at a time. Work French knots on sides and top of crown then finish with a central column of chain stitch and two more rows at the base of the crown. The initials are also worked in stem stitch.

5 Pull bodice down over the neck and backstitch in place around the waist. Cover the raw edges with herringbone to prevent the fabric from fraying.

6 Make the head and attach to the body as described for Ben. Embroider the face and work the hair in the same way. Make an extra bundle of wool and use it to form a moustache, trimming to shape after it has been sewn in place.

MAKING THE CLOTHES

7 Make four identical skirt panels. Turn sides and bottom edges to the front and press. Cover raw edges with braid, taking care to turn the corners neatly.

8 Neaten one long edge of the waist band with a single hem. Gather waist edge of skirt panels and pull up to fit the waist band. Sew in place being careful to match centre front of band between pairs of skirt panels, and have all raw edges level. Fold band upwards and press seam allowance upwards to lie behind the band.

9 Sew gold braid to waist band along top edge of braid only at this stage. (See Fig. b). Turn under each short end of band to wrong side then fold band down to back along the waist line. Now hold all layers together by topstitching through the bottom edge of the braid. Position the skirt on the body around the waist and fasten the edges together at the centre back.

a
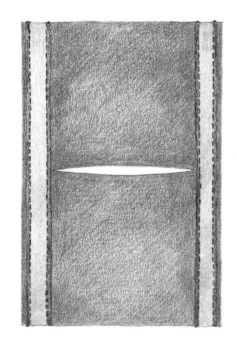

b
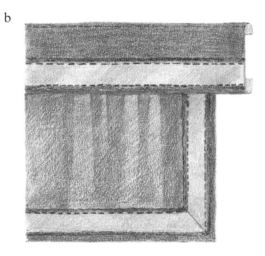

10 Place crown interfacing centrally on wrong side of the hat and stitch together close to the edge. Run a gathering thread around the outer edge of the hat and pull up to fit the brim opening. Make the brim by sewing both pieces right sides together around the outer edge. Have a piece of interfacing against one side of the brim to give it more strength. Trim, turn right side out and topstitch the outer edge. Press the brim. Check that brim opening is large enough to fit on the head.

11 Fit hat sections together and sew. Catch seam allowance to inside of the hat. The stitches will be hidden by the rosettes. Check fit again before proceeding. Position hat on Hal and sew in place covering the hair line.

12 Use the wide, red, blue and white ribbon to make twelve rosettes. There will be four of each colour. Arrange the colours in sequence and sew in place on the hat. An easy solution to this task is to take an extra length of ribbon and sew rosettes to this before fitting the band on the hat and simply catching the edges together. (See Fig. c).

13 More decorative rosettes are used for the shoes and these are made from the three ribbons listed at the end of the materials needed. Cut each ribbon in half and use to make the two rosettes as follows. The red rosettes are identical to those made for the hat. The blue rosettes are similar but smaller in size. Now cut each white ribbon in half again so that you have four lengths. Fold each length to make two loops with ends overlapping in the centre. Arrange two sets of loops at right angles to each other and sew together in the centre. Repeat for the other two sets of loops. Assemble each rosette by sewing white loops to centre of red rosette and then the smaller blue rosette on top of the white. Sew in place on the shoes. (See Fig. d).

14 The neck ruff completes the Tudor costume and is worth the effort and expense of the long ribbon. Gather the entire length along one edge with 12 mm (½ in) stitches. Pull up to fit the neck and sew in place by overlapping and hemming the short ends together at back of the neck. (See Fig. e).

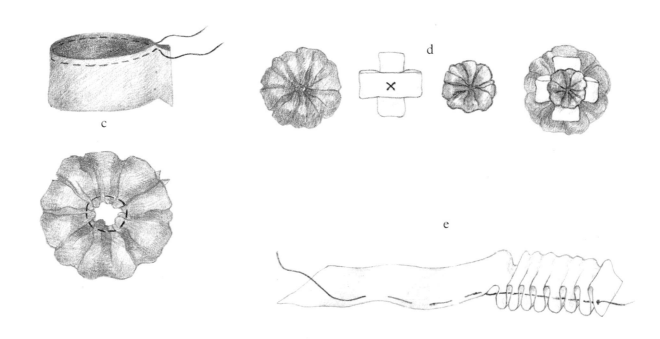

c

d

e

BABY LOVE

Meet Baby Love, the brand-new arrival dressed in her Sunday best angel top. This little darling is easy to love and cuddle. She has painted baby blue eyes, softly rouged cheeks, flaxen curls and will sit up or lie down as you wish. To help you look after her there is a carry cot and to keep her company there is a pattern for a tiny Teddy.

MATERIALS NEEDED TO MAKE DOLL

30 cm × 142 cm (12 in × 56 in) wide flesh coloured stockinette

50 cm (½ yard) stretchy iron-on interfacing

56 g (2 oz) stuffing

Dark brown, blue, black, red and white acrylic paints

5.5 cm × 7.5 cm (2¼ in × 3 in) long vinyl face mask

2 m (2 yards) flaxen coloured acrylic wool

4½ mm (No. 7) knitting needle

Flesh-coloured thread for needle sculpture

Red colouring pencil

Clear all purpose glue

Length of Doll 28 cm (11 in)

MATERIALS NEEDED TO MAKE CLOTHES

A small amount of 3 ply white babywool

3¼ mm (No. 10) knitting needles

56 cm (22 in) white, narrow ribbon

23 cm × 114 cm (9 in × 45 in) wide, fine white embroidery cotton

122 cm (48 in) narrow lace

26.5 cm (10½ in) narrow elastic

A press stud

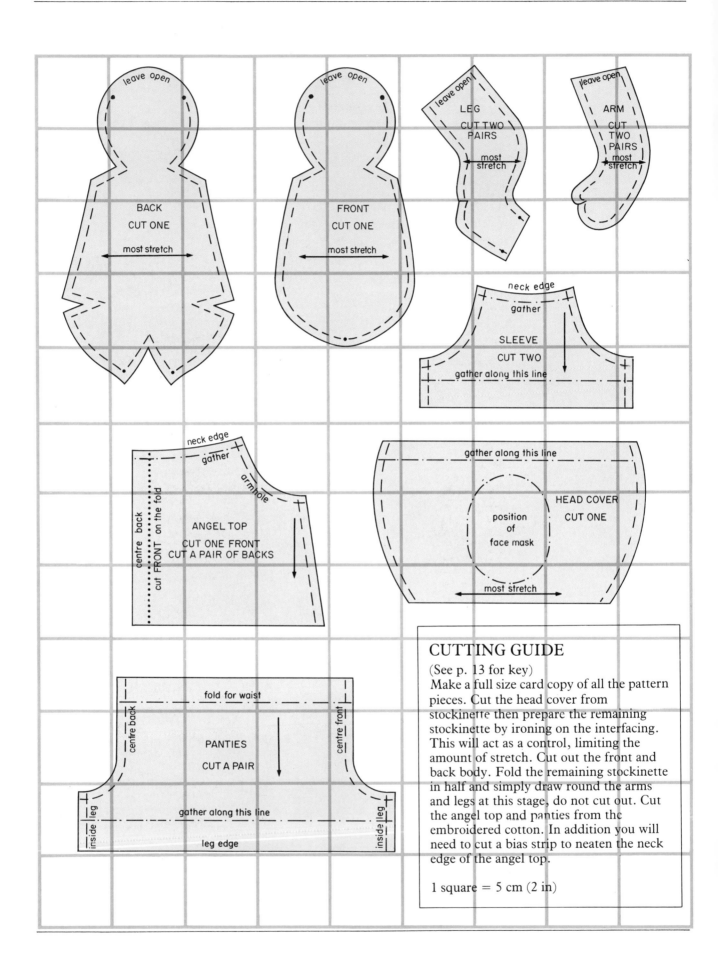

leave open

BACK
CUT ONE

most stretch

leave open

FRONT
CUT ONE

most stretch

leave open

LEG
CUT TWO
PAIRS

most stretch

leave open

ARM
CUT
TWO
PAIRS
most stretch

neck edge

gather

SLEEVE

CUT TWO

gather along this line

neck edge

gather

armhole

centre back

cut FRONT on the fold

ANGEL TOP

CUT ONE FRONT
CUT A PAIR OF BACKS

gather along this line

position
of
face mask

HEAD COVER
CUT ONE

most stretch

fold for waist

centre back

centre front

PANTIES

CUT A PAIR

inside leg

gather along this line

inside leg

leg edge

CUTTING GUIDE

(See p. 13 for key)

Make a full size card copy of all the pattern pieces. Cut the head cover from stockinette then prepare the remaining stockinette by ironing on the interfacing. This will act as a control, limiting the amount of stretch. Cut out the front and back body. Fold the remaining stockinette in half and simply draw round the arms and legs at this stage, do not cut out. Cut the angel top and panties from the embroidered cotton. In addition you will need to cut a bias strip to neaten the neck edge of the angel top.

1 square = 5 cm (2 in)

MAKING THE DOLL

1 The body can be made with narrow seams, 3 mm (⅛ in) as all the edges are protected by the interfacng. Make the three darts on the back and then finger press them open. Sew back to front, leaving open at the top of the head. You will need to ease fullness around the bottom and remember to clip the neck before turning body skin right side out.

2 Stuff the body carefully keeping an awareness of shape. The stretch is around the body and consequently overstuffing will result in a short, dumpy baby. Stuff the head very firmly then close the top. Run a gathering thread around the neck if necessary and pull up to control the fullness.

3 Stitch front and back of each leg in turn, leaving top and bottom straight edges open. Cut legs away from waste material. (See Fig. a). Press open toe edges together so that both seams meet centrally. Sew across the front of the foot, rounding off the corners. Turn leg right side out and stuff firmly, but not hard, to just beyond the knee.

4 Shape the ankles by making a small back stitch on the side then working a long stitch over the front and through the ankle and over the front for a second time. (See Fig. b).

5 Shape toes by working stitches over the edge of the foot. Always start on the underside and lay thread over to the top. One side of the seam will have two toes and the other three. In this way you make a definite large toe. Don't forget to work a right and left foot. (See Fig. c).

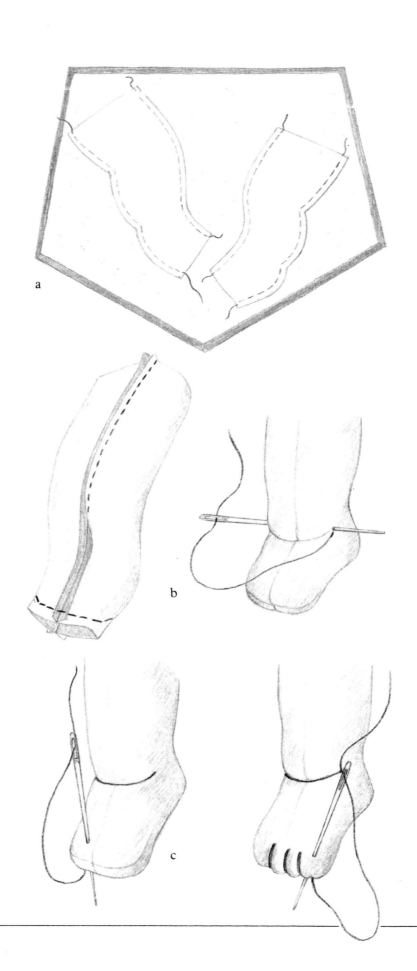

6 Fullness in the sole can be removed by working two dimples. Do this by anchoring the thread in a seam then move the needle to emerge at the side of the ankle. Take a small stitch to the side and down to the dimple, then insert needle at almost the same spot and pass back to the ankle. Pull up forming the dimple and fasten with a small back stitch. Work second dimple from the other side of the ankle. (See Fig. d).

7 Shape the back of the knee in the same way as the ankle then work two dimples on either side of the knee. Turn in the raw edge at the top of the leg and press sides together so that seams are central. Ladderstitch the leg to the body. Make and attach other leg in the same way checking that big toes are in the right position.

8 Lay a long stitch over the dart at the bottom of the back and pass the needle through to the belly button. Pull up to shape the bottom and fasten with a couple of back stitches at the belly button. Now work a circle of small running stitches around the belly button with a diameter of 6 mm (¼ in). Push down in the centre of the circle as you pull up on the thread. Then fasten off invisibly around the belly button.

9 Cover the front of the vinyl face mask with a thin layer of clear all purpose glue, making sure that it covers the features. Wait a few minutes for the glue to become tacky then gently lower the head cover on to the mask. Use the sides of your little fingers to gently press the fabric into the eye sockets, sides of nose, mouth and chin so that the features are clearly defined. Leave to dry.

10 Fold up lower edge behind the mask and then pin the head cover directly into the shoulder seams of the body. Continue pinning folded edge all round the neck to the back. Turn under raw edges at back and ladderstitch the curved centre back seam up to the top of the head. Readjust pins around the neck if necessary to spread fullness then stitch in place. There should not be any need to stitch under the chin as the mask should hold the fold in place. (See Fig. e).

11 Stuff head, achieving a good shape and inserting stuffing between mask and inner head to push face forward. Gather up the top edge of the head, turn raw edges in and pull up and fasten off.

12 Sew arms together round curved edges leaving top open. Cut away from waste material and turn right side out. Stuff each arm lightly. Turn in top edge and oversew sides together. Lay arm over shoulder and sew in place with thumb towards the front. Finish second arm in the same way.

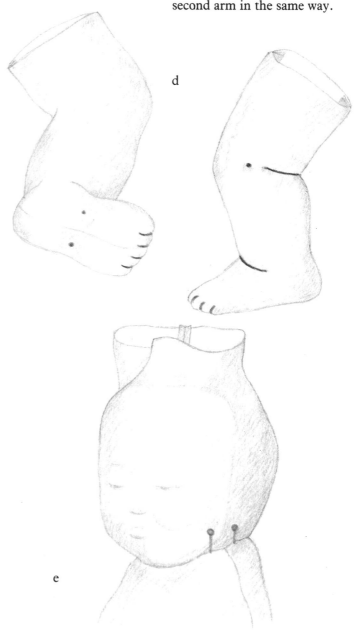

d

e

13 Make curls in the same way as described for the Gingham Girls (p. 60) by winding wool over the needle and stemstitching in place. Make a length of continuous curl. Centre curls on the forehead and backstitch one half around the face on one side and then snake it backwards and forwards over the side of the head. Cover the other half of the head with the remaining length of curl.

14 Paint the bed of the eyes with white. Leave to dry and if necessary paint again to get a good base to work on. This foundation must be absolutely dry before painting the blue iris which in turn must be dry before the black pupil can be painted.

15 With a fine brush, work a thin dark brown line over the top of the eye then stroke out a few, very fine eyelashes. Lightly paint the eyebrows. Finally, add a white dot to each pupil, and a red spot on the inside corner of the eyes. Colour the cheeks and the mouth with red pencil held sideways so that colour is added slowly, rather like rouging.

MAKING THE PANTIES

16 Sew centre front and centre back seams, trim and clip curves. Make a narrow double hem on each leg edge. Decorate with lace. Work two rows of gathering across each leg and pull up to approximately 14 cm (5½ in). Machine stitch across the gathers to make them secure.

17 Turn down waist edge to make a casing for the elastic. Topstitch the fold and then feed the elastic through the channel. Sew ends together and close channel opening. Join the inside legs with a french seam. Turn panties right side out and dress on Baby Love.

MAKING THE ANGEL TOP

18 Make a narrow double hem on each sleeve edge. Decorate with lace. Work two rows of gathering across each sleeve and pull up to fit the arms, loosely. Machine across gathers to make them secure. (See Fig. f).

19 Sew sleeves to armhole edges of front and backs. Now fold each sleeve in turn to bring underarm edges together and the sides. Sew underarm and side seam continuously. Clip corner to release tension. Turn angel top to right side and hem both back edges and the lower edge.

20 Gather all round the neck edge and pull up to fit Baby Love. Remember to leave a small overlap. Neaten neck edge with a bias strip and then decorate with lace. Sew a press stud at the back opening then dress on to dolly.

MAKING THE BOOTEES

21 Cast on 17 stitches. Knit 4 rows. Next row – knit 1 * yarn forward, knit 2 together, repeat from * to end. Next row – purl.
Divide for foot as follows: knit 11, turn, knit 5, turn, knit 8 rows on these 5 stitches, break yarn. Rejoin yarn to inside group of stitches left on right hand needle. With right hand side facing knit up 5 stitches along side of foot, knit across 5 stitches on needle, knit up 5 stitches along other side of foot then knit across remaining 6 stitches (27 stitches): Knit 3 rows.
Shape foot as follows: Row 1: (knit 1, knit 2 together, knit 8, knit 2 together) twice, knit 1.
Row 2: knit 1, knit 2 together, knit to last 3 stitches, knit 2 together, knit 1.
Row 3: (knit 1, knit 2 together, knit 5, knit 2 together), twice, knit 1. Cast off. Make up each bootee and thread ribbon through holes at ankle.

f

BABY LOVE'S CARRY COT AND TEDDY

Here is a carry cot to help you look after your Baby Love. It is just the right size for young mothers, designed with sensible handles to carry it by when travelling out and about. Tuck the handles under the mattress and you have a soft sculptured bed with a quilt and pillow to complete the bedding. And sitting here waiting for dolly is her very own Teddy.

MATERIALS NEEDED

100 cm × 114 cm (36 in × 45 in) wide dark blue cotton

100 cm × 114 cm (36 in × 45 in) wide pale blue cotton

100 cm × 92 cm (36 in × 36 in) wide polyester batting

137 cm (1½ yards) of 25 mm (1 in) wide broderie anglaise

107 cm (42 in) of 50 mm (2 in) wide broderie anglaise

A scrap of teddy coloured fleecy courtelle

2 small black beads for eyes

A small amount of ribbon for neck bow

150 g (6 oz) stuffing

Length of Carry Cot 35.5 cm (14 in)   Height of Teddy 10 cm (4 in)

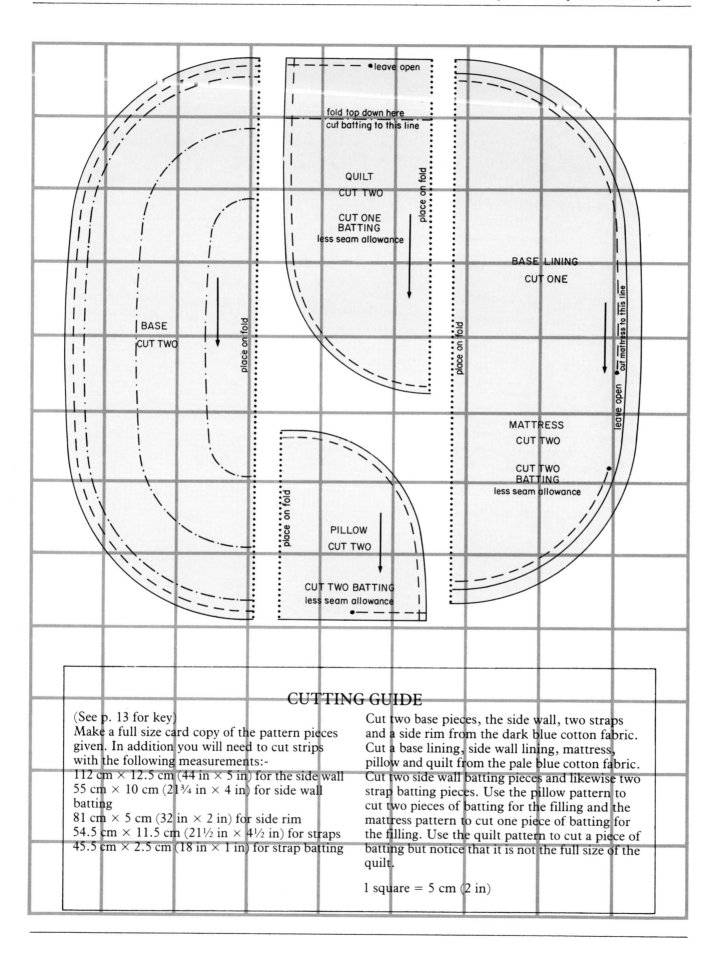

CUTTING GUIDE

(See p. 13 for key)
Make a full size card copy of the pattern pieces given. In addition you will need to cut strips with the following measurements:-

112 cm × 12.5 cm (44 in × 5 in) for the side wall
55 cm × 10 cm (21¾ in × 4 in) for side wall batting
81 cm × 5 cm (32 in × 2 in) for side rim
54.5 cm × 11.5 cm (21½ in × 4½ in) for straps
45.5 cm × 2.5 cm (18 in × 1 in) for strap batting

Cut two base pieces, the side wall, two straps and a side rim from the dark blue cotton fabric. Cut a base lining, side wall lining, mattress, pillow and quilt from the pale blue cotton fabric. Cut two side wall batting pieces and likewise two strap batting pieces. Use the pillow pattern to cut two pieces of batting for the filling and the mattress pattern to cut one piece of batting for the filling. Use the quilt pattern to cut a piece of batting but notice that it is not the full size of the quilt.

1 square = 5 cm (2 in)

MAKING THE CARRY COT

1 Lay both base pieces together, right sides out, and sew round the edges. Now tack all round 12 mm (½ in) inside the edge. This row of tacking will make it easier to sew the base to the side wall by keeping the stuffing away from the foot of the machine.

2 Sew along the two inner rows marked on the pattern. These rows divide the base into three separate areas for stuffing. Now make a slit through one layer only, centrally in each of the areas on the long axis. This results in two slits in both the outer and middle areas and one slit in the centre. Stuff the base firmly then close each slit in turn with herringbone stitch. Lay the base lining, face upwards, over the slit side of the base and tack in place round the edge. The base is now complete. (See Fig. a).

3 Sew short ends of the side wall together and press seam open. Prepare side wall lining in the same way. Feed lining inside the outer wall with wrong sides together and seams matching. Sew bottom edges together and topstitch through the wall seam. Fold wall in half to determine the opposite point to the seam then topstitch through both layers at this point to divide the wall in half.

4 Insert a piece of batting in each half and push down to the bottom then tack in place. Now refold the wall to find quarter points and topstitch each in turn. Refold again to divide the quarters then topstitch and continue in the same way until you have divided the wall into sixteen channels. (See Fig. b).

5 Sew base to lower edge of the side wall, easing wall to fit. Do this by hand if the bulk proves difficult for you to manage on the machine. Trim raw edges and then neaten by oversewing the raw edges or covering with purchased bias binding. Remove tacking stitches from the base.

a

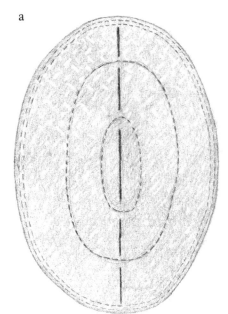

6 Turn the carry cot right side out and insert a small amount of stuffing into each channel of the wall between the lining and the batting. This will pull the sides in and give them more strength. Tack top edges together and then tack the wide broderie anglaise to the top with raw edges level. Now gather up the edge to 76 cm (30 in) to reduce the opening by pulling the sides in.

7 Join short ends of rim together and press seam flat. Turn carry cot wrong side out and with right sides together and raw edges level join rim to wall, trapping lace between.

8 Bring the rim over the top edge to the inside of the carry cot, turn under the raw edge and hem in place to the wall inserting stuffing as you work. This will pad out the rim, making a firm, rolled edge. (See Fig. c).

b

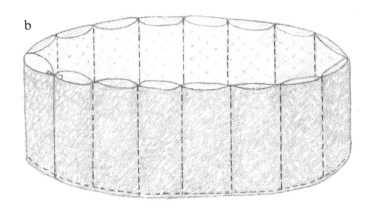

c

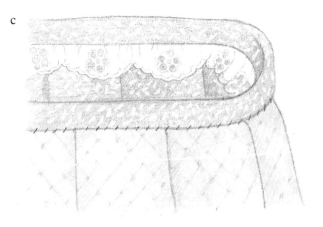

9 Take a fabric strap piece and press under a narrow turning on both short ends and one long side. Lay strip batting centrally on the wrong side of the strap. Fold first the long raw edge over the batting then the neatened side. Sew along the strap to hold the folds in place. Make a second strap in the same way.

10 Place each strap against the inside wall with short edges down at the base. Sew in place. Sew straps to inside of the rim to make them more secure. (See Fig. d).

MAKING THE MATTRESS

11 Sew mattress pieces together leaving a small opening on the side. Turn right side out. Trim batting to fit mattress then fold to put inside mattress. Open out flat and close opening with ladder stitch. Place mattress in the bottom of the carry cot.

MAKING THE PILLOW

12 Cut a length of narrow lace a little longer than the curve of the pillow. Gather it up and tack to curve of one pillow piece with raw edges level. Lay second pillow piece on top with right sides together and seam round edge leaving a small opening on the straight edge. Turn pillow right side out.

13 Trim both batting pieces to fit then fold and insert inside pillow. Open batting out flat and puff up the pillow by placing a small amount of stuffing between the two layers. Close the opening and put the pillow in the bed.

MAKING THE QUILT

14 Gather edge of lace and tack all around the edge of one quilt side with raw edges level. Lay second quilt piece on top with right sides together and sew all round the edge leaving a small opening on the top, straight edge. Turn quilt right side out and insert batting. Close opening then fold top edge of quilt over to outside and catch it down on both sides.

d

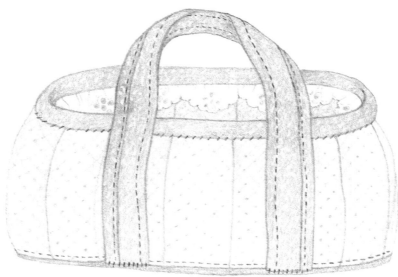

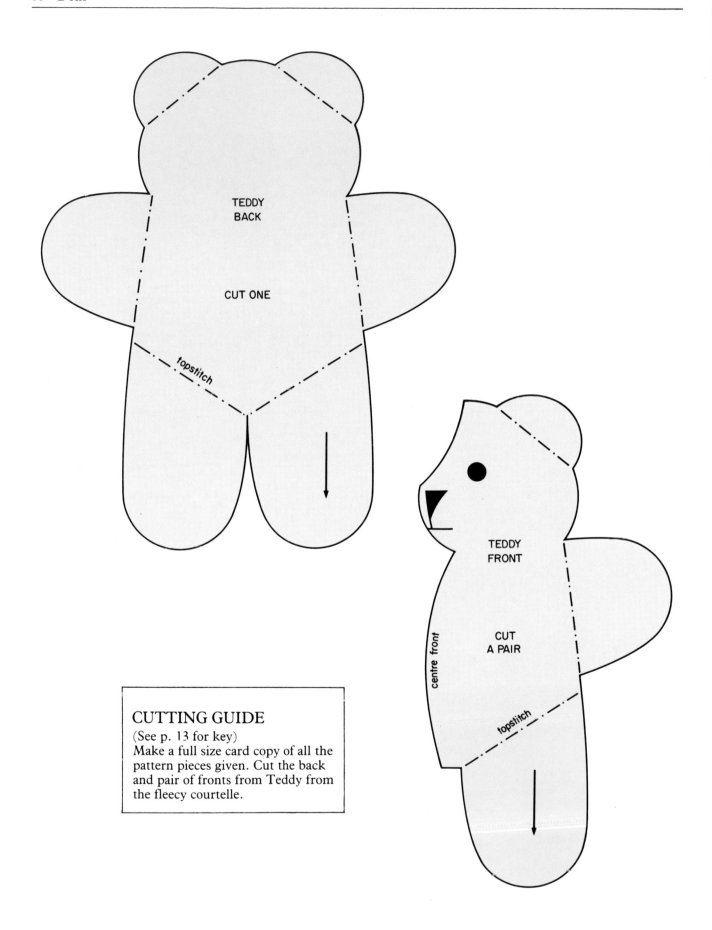

TEDDY
BACK

CUT ONE

topstitch

TEDDY
FRONT

centre front

CUT
A PAIR

topstitch

CUTTING GUIDE
(See p. 13 for key)
Make a full size card copy of all the
pattern pieces given. Cut the back
and pair of fronts from Teddy from
the fleecy courtelle.

MAKING THE TEDDY

1 Using the narrowest seam possible, join the fronts together along the centre front seam. Join front to back, leaving a small opening along one side of a leg. Now turn Teddy right side out and stabstitch across the base of each ear.

2 Fill the head then arms, far leg, tummy and leg nearest the opening. Close the opening. Teddy may be rather fat at this stage so wind a thread around the neck to give him more shape. Then stabstitch across the tops of the arms and legs so that they can bend.

3 Sew eyes in place securely, or embroider them if Teddy is going to a very young child. Work a satin stitch nose and straight stitch mouth as outlined for the Acrobats (p. 30). Finish Teddy by tying a bow around the neck. (See Fig. a).

a

GLOBAL CHILDREN

*These barefoot toddlers represent the children of the world. The pattern is
for a basic rag doll that can be styled to give quite different effects.*

MATERIALS NEEDED FOR EACH DOLL

46 cm × 114 cm (18 in × 45 in) wide
firm weave cotton, viyella or
curtain lining in appropriate skin
colour

280 g (10 oz) stuffing

15 cm × 40 cm (6 in × 16 in) wide
long pile blond fur for Gretchen

15 cm × 40 cm (6 in × 16 in) wide
long pile black fur for Liu Lee

A 12 mm knitting needle

26 g (1 oz) black bobbly wool

Acrylic paints, white, brown and
black

Embroidery thread for mouth

Black or dark brown sewing thread
to outline eyes

Blush powder

Height of each Doll 46 cm (18 in)

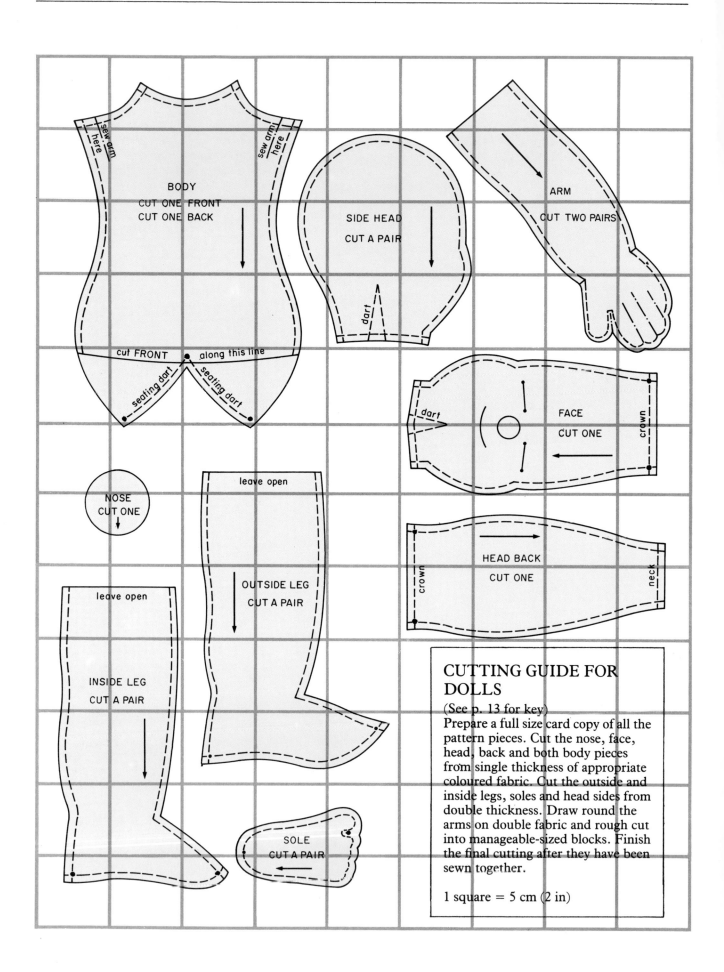

BODY
CUT ONE FRONT
CUT ONE BACK

sew arm here

sew arm here

cut FRONT along this line

seating dart

seating dart

SIDE HEAD
CUT A PAIR

dart

ARM
CUT TWO PAIRS

dart

FACE
CUT ONE

crown

NOSE
CUT ONE

crown

HEAD BACK
CUT ONE

neck

leave open

OUTSIDE LEG
CUT A PAIR

leave open

INSIDE LEG
CUT A PAIR

SOLE
CUT A PAIR

CUTTING GUIDE FOR DOLLS
(See p. 13 for key)
Prepare a full size card copy of all the pattern pieces. Cut the nose, face, head, back and both body pieces from single thickness of appropriate coloured fabric. Cut the outside and inside legs, soles and head sides from double thickness. Draw round the arms on double fabric and rough cut into manageable-sized blocks. Finish the final cutting after they have been sewn together.

1 square = 5 cm (2 in)

MAKING THE DOLLS

1 Sew the seating dart in the lower half of the back body. Place the front and back right sides together and sew down each side in turn, leaving neck and bottom open.

2 Make the darts in the side head pieces and under the chin on the face. Sew face to head back across the crown. Now carefully fit the face between the side heads taking care to keep rounded cheeks and tack in place. Fit head back between the sides, matching the neck edge and easing any fullness towards the crown where it will be hidden by the hair. Trim seams.

3 Turn the completed head right side out and push down through the neck opening of the body. Match chin dart to centre front of body and check that the head is set level. Sew in place. This may be easier to accomplish by hand sewing using a small back stitch. Turn completed body skin right side out and set aside.

4 Sew an inside leg to matching outside leg down the back to the heel and then down the front to the toes. Insert sole, taking care to align the match points. Press the front leg seam open at the match point and sew a slit to separate the big toe from the rest. Clip down inside edge of the big toe then turn leg right side out and stuff firmly, nearly to the top. Hold stuffing in place with a pin. (See Fig. a). Make the second leg in the same way, checking that you have made a pair.

5 Work the remaining toes by oversewing toe divisions with doubled thread that matches the colour of the fabric. Pull up on the stitches and this will make lovely little chubby toes, too delightful to be hidden away inside socks and shoes.

6 Position the legs against the lower front edge of the body with all the raw edges level and toes pointing upwards towards the chin. Check that big toes are together in the centre then sew in place. Remove pins that are holding the stuffing in place.

7 Stuff the head firmly to achieve a good, solid shape. Take a long needle with strong, doubled thread and work from inside the neck to emerge at the bottom corner of an eye. Take the thread across the base of the eye to the other corner and then pass the needle back down to the inside of the neck. Remove needle from thread. Pull up on threads and knot both ends together securely. This will sink the eye into the face, forming a socket and make the cheeks appear to protrude. (See Fig. b). Work the second eye in the same way. (Liu Lee does not have these stitches, thus keeping her face flat and very round.)

8 Continue stuffing the remainder of the body, filling out the shoulders and the bottom. Close body by ladderstitching to the back of the legs. Sew round arm starting at the top edge with a normal seam allowance and narrow down to a 3 mm (⅛ in) seam around the fingers. Sew a deep slit between thumb and fingers, squaring off at the bottom rather than making a 'V'. Cut arm away from waste fabric. Clip into slit. Turn the arm right side out and stuff the hand area lightly. Hold the stuffing in place by pinning across the wrist. Make the second arm in the same way to this point so that you can embroider fingers at the same time and make a matching pair.

9 Separate the fingers by pinning in the appropriate place then stabstitch down the divisions in turn. Remove the pin at the wrist and finish stuffing the arm firmly up to approximately 3.5 cm (1½ in) from the top. Pin to hold the stuffing in place. Turn in raw edges at top and oversew sides together. Finish other arm in same way. (See Fig. c).

10 Lay each arm in turn across a shoulder having hands level with the tops of the legs and both thumbs facing forward. Sew in place. Remove pins, holding the stuffing in place, and reshape arms by stroking with your fingers to relocate the stuffing so that the arms hang down beside the body instead of standing out.

11 Further shaping of the arms can be achieved by reducing the thickness at the wrist. Work a row of ladder stitch across the inside wrist starting with shallow stitches and widening in the middle before becoming shallow on the opposite sides. This surface worked dart will turn the hand inwards in a gentle gesture. Work on the outside of the arm and the hand will lift up.

a

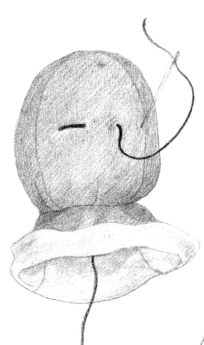

b

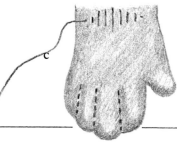

c

MAKING THE FACE

12 All the toddlers have the same basic face with just slight differences in the size of the eyes necessitated by the amount of stretch in the skin fabric. Start by painting each eye with a bed of white paint. Set aside to dry thoroughly before painting the brown iris and dry again before finishing with the black pupil. Finally, add a white highlight.

13 Use black or dark brown sewing thread to outline each eye with stem stitch and a few short straight stitch eye lashes. Finish with short eyebrows worked in stem stitch. Blush cheeks and nose with face powder.

14 The mouth is worked in stem stitch and may be either a simple curve for a smile or have upper lips added as two upside-down fly stitches and a lower lip as a very short line. Blusher over the lips can help impart the same colouring.

MAKING THE HAIR

15 The toddlers have two different hairstyles between them, one using long pile fur to make a wig cap of straight hair and the other using wool to make curls. Liu Lee and Gretchen have wig caps made in the same way. Only the colour and final styling are different. Make the darts on each side in turn by bringing A to B and seaming, then work C to B in the same way. Sew the short edges A/C to D. Fold wig in half and sew centre front dart and continue down the centre back to the bottom edge. (See Fig. d).

16 Turn wig right side out and gently pull on to the head, being careful not to trap any fur under the edge. Check that the seam lies centrally at the back and that the hair line over the brow is correctly placed. Hem wig in place.

17 Groom the wig by brushing down towards the face and neck and releasing any fur trapped in the seams on the crown. Liu Lee has a truly simple style with the fur over the eyes being trimmed short to make a fringe. (If you were to make a Chinese boy instead, then follow the line marked on the pattern for short hair and trim all ends short.) Gretchen has a side parting. This is achieved by brushing the fur away from the parting line required.

18 Sarah's curls are made by winding wool round the 12 mm needle and stemstitching them together as described for the Gingham Girls (p. 60). You will need to make 2 m (6 ft 6 in) of curls. Centre the curls on the forehead and sew them in place by snaking them over the head and backstitching in place.

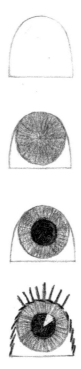

d

LIU LEE

Liu Lee is a Chinese girl wearing the familiar dark blue jacket with traditional frog fastenings. Her wig is quickly made from shiny black fur fabric.

MATERIALS NEEDED FOR CLOTHES

46 cm × 92 cm (18 in × 36 in) wide navy blue cotton
76 cm (30 in) of 1.5 cm (¾ in) wide black tape
61 cm (24 in) black bias binding
33 cm × 92 cm (13 in × 36 in) wide floral print cotton
61 cm × 92 cm (24 in × 36 in) wide brightly coloured cotton
61 cm (24 in) narrow cotton lace to decorate dress
152 cm (5 ft) narrow elastic
75 cm × 92 cm (30 in × 36 in) wide white cotton
23 cm × 92 cm (9 in × 36 in) wide embroidered white cotton
152 cm (5 ft) narrow braid for dirndl
92 cm (36 in) cotton lace for petticoat
hook and eye for dirndl
four snap fasteners for blouse and dress

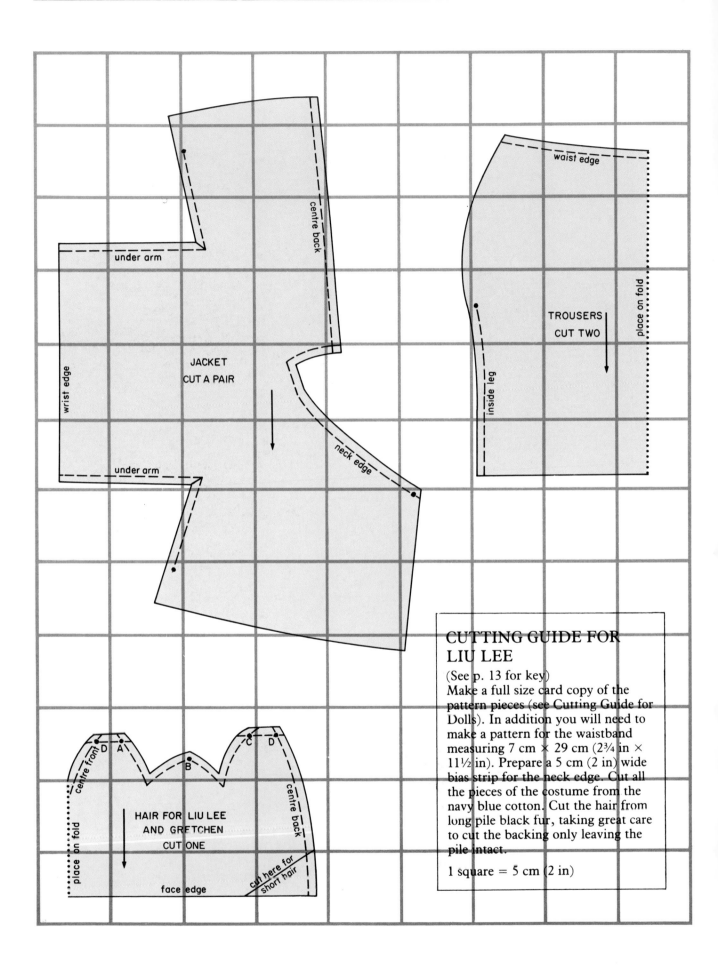

under arm

centre back

wrist edge

JACKET
CUT A PAIR

neck edge

under arm

waist edge

place on fold

TROUSERS
CUT TWO

inside leg

centre front

D A

C D

B

centre back

HAIR FOR LIU LEE
AND GRETCHEN

CUT ONE

place on fold

cut here for
short hair

face edge

CUTTING GUIDE FOR LIU LEE

(See p. 13 for key)
Make a full size card copy of the pattern pieces (see Cutting Guide for Dolls). In addition you will need to make a pattern for the waistband measuring 7 cm × 29 cm (2¾ in × 11½ in). Prepare a 5 cm (2 in) wide bias strip for the neck edge. Cut all the pieces of the costume from the navy blue cotton. Cut the hair from long pile black fur, taking great care to cut the backing only leaving the pile intact.

1 square = 5 cm (2 in)

MAKING THE CLOTHES FOR LIU LEE

1 Hem each side of both trouser legs from the waist down to the match point. Sew inside leg seams from match point down to ankle edge. Turn the legs right side out and place them side by side with a small overlap in the centre of the waist. Gather waist from side to side and pull up to fit the doll.

2 Make a single, narrow hem on one long edge of the waist band. Place other long edge against waist of trousers with right sides together and raw edges level. Sew. Press seam and waistband upwards. Turn in short ends of waistband then fold the waistband down to inside of trousers with edge lying below the seam line. Working on the right side, topstitch along the waist just below the waistbad. This is known as 'stitching in the ditch' and is how the necks of the dress and blouse are finished for the Global Children. (See Fig. a).

3 Hem ankle edges at required length. Cut black tape in half and sew to each side of the waistband. Fit trousers on Liu Lee and pass tapes around waist and tie in bow. Tuck ends in side trousers.

4 Sew jacket together at centre back. Hem both wrist edges. Hem lower back edge between match points on each side seam. Now hem each front edge, lower edge and up to match point on side seam in turn.

5 Neaten the neck edge and front cross overs with the wide bias strip. Finish by hemming the bias strip to the seam line on the wrong side. Fold jacket in half across the shoulders then sew each underarm and side seam in turn down to the match points, leaving the slits open at the bottom. Clip the armpits, turn jacket right side out and press.

6 Take the black bias binding, fold in half and stitch the edges together. Cut two 10 cm (4 in) lengths for the loops and two 20 cm (8 in) lengths for the knots. Make a loop by folding the strip in half and pressing the end flat into an arrowhead. Turn raw edges under and sew loop to front of jacket so that it projects over the edge. Make second loop in the same way and sew to front of jacket just above the waist level. (See Fig. b).

7 To make the knotted half of the frogs fold to find the centre point of the strip. Tie a knot in the centre then three more knots on top of it forming a tight ball. Form the ball by pressing and working the knots with your fingers. Turn under raw edges and sew on jacket front opposite corresponding loop. Dress Liu Lee in her jacket. (See Fig. c).

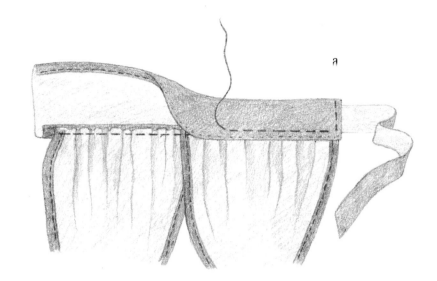

a

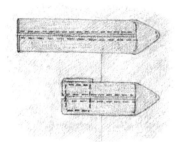

b

c

GRETCHEN

Gretchen is a mid-European lassie with her dirndl skirt, peasant blouse and eyelet embroidered apron. Felt bolero and boots could easily be added to extend her wardrobe.

MATERIALS NEEDED FOR GRETCHEN'S CLOTHES

33 cm × 92 cm (13 in × 36 in) wide floral print cotton

23 cm × 92 cm (9 in × 36 in) wide embroidered white cotton

152 cm (5 ft) narrow braid for dirndl

Hook and eye for dirndl

2 snap fasteners for blouse

75 cm × 92 cm (30 in × 36 in) wide white cotton

92 cm (36 in) cotton lace for petticoat

92 cm (36 in) narrow elastic

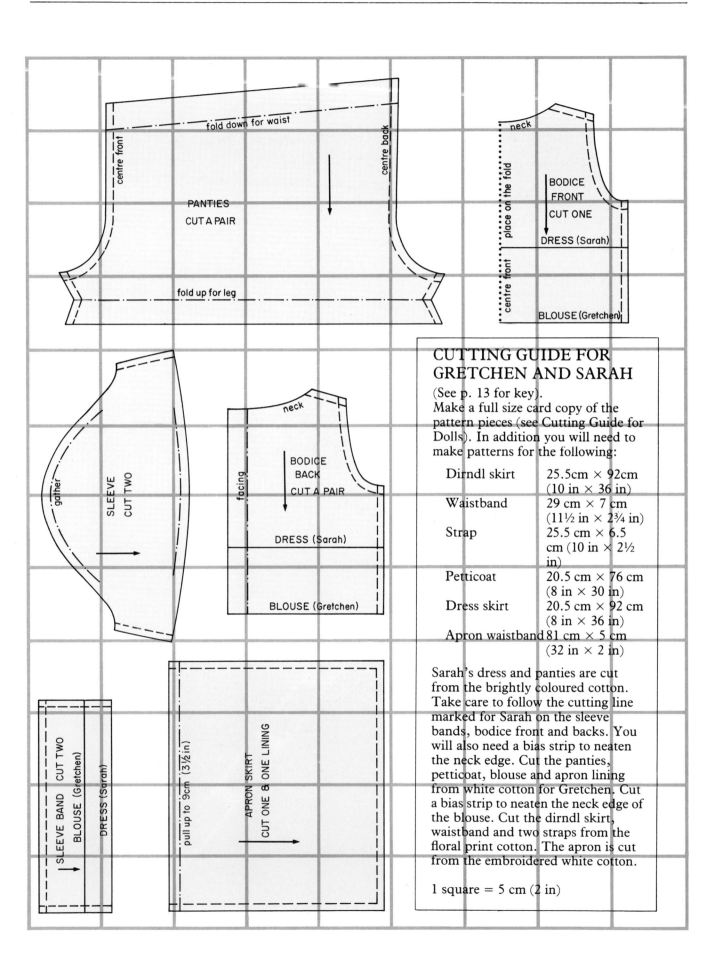

PANTIES
CUT A PAIR

centre front

centre back

fold down for waist

fold up for leg

neck

place on the fold

centre front

BODICE
FRONT
CUT ONE
DRESS (Sarah)

BLOUSE (Gretchen)

gather

SLEEVE
CUT TWO

facing

neck

BODICE
BACK
CUT A PAIR

DRESS (Sarah)

BLOUSE (Gretchen)

SLEEVE BAND CUT TWO
BLOUSE (Gretchen)
DRESS (Sarah)

pull up to 9cm (3½ in)

APRON SKIRT
CUT ONE & ONE LINING

CUTTING GUIDE FOR GRETCHEN AND SARAH

(See p. 13 for key).
Make a full size card copy of the pattern pieces (see Cutting Guide for Dolls). In addition you will need to make patterns for the following:

Dirndl skirt	25.5cm × 92cm (10 in × 36 in)
Waistband	29 cm × 7 cm (11½ in × 2¾ in)
Strap	25.5 cm × 6.5 cm (10 in × 2½ in)
Petticoat	20.5 cm × 76 cm (8 in × 30 in)
Dress skirt	20.5 cm × 92 cm (8 in × 36 in)
Apron waistband	81 cm × 5 cm (32 in × 2 in)

Sarah's dress and panties are cut from the brightly coloured cotton. Take care to follow the cutting line marked for Sarah on the sleeve bands, bodice front and backs. You will also need a bias strip to neaten the neck edge. Cut the panties, petticoat, blouse and apron lining from white cotton for Gretchen. Cut a bias strip to neaten the neck edge of the blouse. Cut the dirndl skirt, waistband and two straps from the floral print cotton. The apron is cut from the embroidered white cotton.

1 square = 5 cm (2 in)

MAKING THE CLOTHES FOR GRETCHEN

1 Make the panties as described for Sarah. Sew the short sides of the petticoat together with a narrow French seam. Make a narrow turning to the front on one long edge. Turn under the raw edge of the cotton lace then cover the petticoat fold with the lace and topstitch the two together. (See Fig. a). This is the lower edge of the half slip.

2 Make a narrow turning on the waist edge then fold over by 2 cm (¾ in) and topstitch the fold close to the edge. Topstitch neatened edge forming a casing but remember to leave a small opening at the back. Thread 25 cm (10 in) elastic through the casing, check fit before sewing ends together and closing the opening.

3 The blouse is made in much the same way as the bodice for Sarah's dress. However, instead of having a pleat at the front, the excess width is softly gathered at the neck edge. Also there is no lace decorating the sleeves and the sleeve band is narrower.

4 The dirndl is made by sewing the short ends together leaving an opening at one end for the waist. Neaten back opening on both sides. Gather waist and sew to waistband in the same way as the waistband of Liu Lee's trousers. Fit a hook and eye at the opening. Hem dirndl to required length then decorate skirt with a narrow band of colourful braid or ribbon.

5 Make each strap by folding in half lengthways and sewing edges. Turn right side out and press flat with seam at centre back of the strap. Decorate front of strap with braid. Sew each end of straps to inside of the waistband.

6 Sew apron skirt and lining together down both sides and across the bottom. Clip the corners off, turn right side out and press. Gather up waist edge to 9 cm (3½ in). Prepare band by pressing a narrow turning on both long sides. Locate centre of band and place waist edge of apron centrally against one long edge with raw edges level. Tack in place.

7 Fold band in half, turn in short ends then topstitch edges of band together. Press all clothes and put dress on Gretchen.

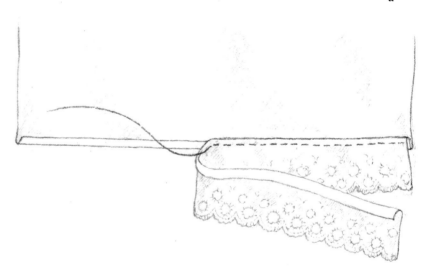

a

SARAH

*Sarah is a cosmopolitan child who could just as easily
be from the Americas or Africa. Choose a brightly coloured
fabric to complement her lovely dark colouring and
finish her with yarn curls.*

MATERIALS NEEDED FOR SARAH'S CLOTHES

61 cm × 92 cm (24 in × 36 in) wide
   brightly coloured cotton
2 snap fasteners for dress
61 cm (24 in) narrow cotton lace to
   decorate dress
61 cm (24 in) narrow elastic

MAKING THE CLOTHES FOR SARAH

1 Make a hem on each leg edge wide enough to take the elastic. Topstitch both sides of the casing. Thread a 17.5 cm (7 in) length of elastic through each casing and stitch each end securely to hold.

2 Place both sections of panties right sides together and sew centre back and centre front seams in turn. Sew inside leg edges making sure that the elastic is securely caught within the seams.

3 Fold down waist and make a casing for the elastic, leaving a small opening at the back. Again topstitch both sides of the channel. Thread a 25 cm (10 in) length of elastic through the waist, check fit on Sarah before fastening ends togethr. Close opening, press panties, then dress on Sarah.

4 Fold front bodice piece in half with right sides out and sew 12 mm (½ in) behind the fold. Press fold flat to make a box pleat. Cut two pieces of lace to fit from neck to waist and sew one each side of the pleat with the base of the lace behind the pleat. Sew front and backs together across the shoulders. (See Fig. a).

5 Gather each sleeve head in turn and sew into armhole openings of bodice. Gather elbow edges. Sew bands to wrong side of sleeves. Turn bands forward to front of sleeves and hem or topstitch in place trapping lace in the seam. (See Fig. b). Sew underarm and side seam on each side. Trim seam and clip the corners.

6 Gather waist edge of skirt and pull up to fit the bodice. Adjust the gathers, spreading the fullness evenly, and seam. Hem the back edges and neaten the neck edge with a bias strip. Sew on snap fasteners. Fit dress on Sarah to determine the length and finish by hemming then pressing.

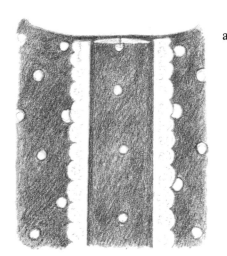

a

b

ANIMALS

Elephants, camels, monkeys, horses and pigs were among the first animals to be commercially made as soft toys and remain just as popular and topical today as they were in the 1880s when they were first introduced. These early toys were produced by the German firm Steiff and were made of felt with black shoe button eyes—materials that have been largely replaced in the twentieth century by mohair and glass eyes and, more recently, by knitted furs and plastic safety eyes.

Bears are unquestionably the all-time favourites and yet they only appeared on the market as Teddys just over eighty years ago. There is a rival claim for the first design of a stand-up bear but the name 'Teddy' was undoubtedly inspired by the American President Theodore Roosevelt. His family were further involved with bears when his two sons, Theodore Jnr and Kermit, visited China in 1928 and caught several Pandas. At this time Pandas were still relatively unknown to the Western world and it was not until the late 1930s, after the animals appeared in Chicago, New York and London Zoo, that the craze for Pandas really began. Today, fifty years later, Pandas are firmly established alongside Teddys in the toybox.

Other animals to add to your collection of soft toys are the cuddly baby owls and penguin together with a very appealing seal. Gilbert, with his long gangling limbs, will provide many hours of fun for boys and girls alike as will Bumbles who is more of a bear than a Teddy. Lastly there is Dorinda the dragon, a really splendid soft toy for a very discerning little owner who still believes in the magic of dragonland.

THE OWLETTS

Barny and Snowball are two delightfully fluffy baby owls, a fluffiness that is achieved by using a good-quality dense, medium pile length fur. Anything less and the owletts would lose their youthfulness. Instructions are given for making Snowball as Barny is merely a colour variation, using beige fur for the body, cream for the face mask and brown felt for the feet and beak.

MATERIALS NEEDED

23 cm × 138 cm (9 in × 54 in) wide
   white medium pile fur
15 cm (6 in) square of grey felt
56 g (2 oz) stuffing
A pair of 18 mm brown safety eyes

Height of Owlett 15 cm (6 in)

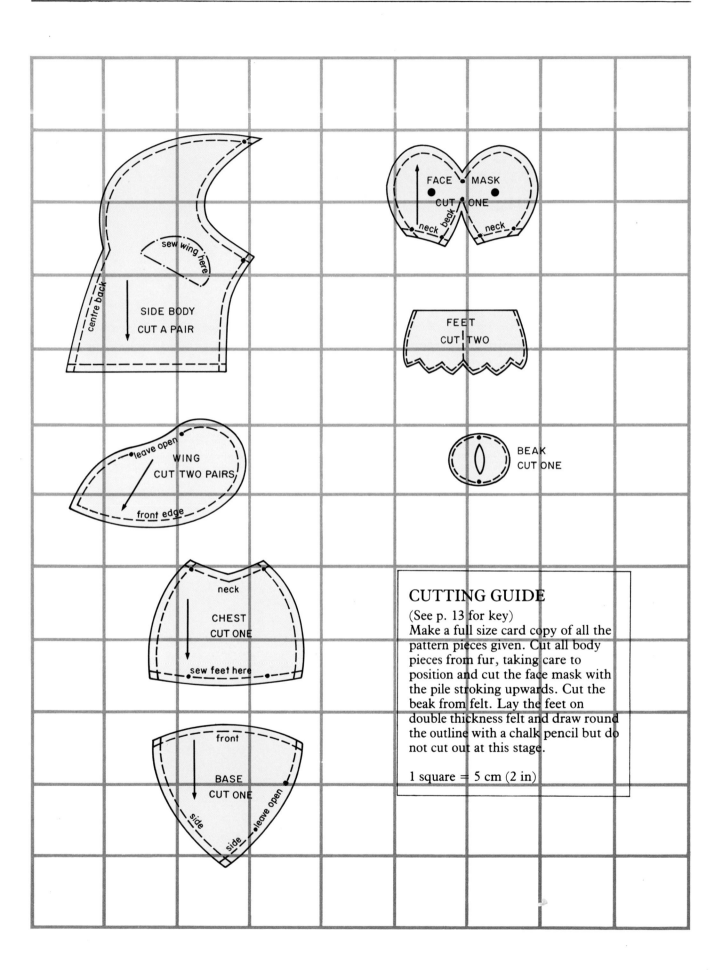

sew wing here

centre back

SIDE BODY
CUT A PAIR

leave open

WING
CUT TWO PAIRS

front edge

neck

CHEST
CUT ONE

sew feet here

front

BASE
CUT ONE

side

side leave open

FACE • MASK
CUT ONE

neck beak neck

FEET
CUT TWO

BEAK
CUT ONE

CUTTING GUIDE

(See p. 13 for key)
Make a full size card copy of all the
pattern pieces given. Cut all body
pieces from fur, taking care to
position and cut the face mask with
the pile stroking upwards. Cut the
beak from felt. Lay the feet on
double thickness felt and draw round
the outline with a chalk pencil but do
not cut out at this stage.

1 square = 5 cm (2 in)

1 Fold the beak in half with wrong sides together and stabstitch close to the outer curved edge. Stuff firmly through the small central slit then oversew the beak to one side of the dart before closing the dart. (See Figs. a and b).

2 Sew the face mask to the chest, completing the front of the body. Now sew a side body to each side of the front in turn. Start at the neck and follow round the curve of the face to the brow. (This is more successfully done by handsewing rather than by machine.) Complete the seam by sewing down from the neck to the base. Fold body to bring centre back edges together and sew from the brow down to the base.

3 Turn the body right side out and fix the safety eyes in place. Topstitch the feet together just inside the chalk line, leaving the straight edge open. Brush away the chalk line then cut out the feet. Stuff each foot towards the toes only then baste to the lower edge of the chest with the toes pointing towards the neck. Turn body wrong side out. (See Fig. c).

4 Sew base in place leaving an opening on one side. Turn completed skin right side out and carefully stuff a soft rounded shape. Close opening with ladder stitch.

5 Tack a pair of wing pieces together, taking care to tuck in the fur at the tip. Sew, leaving a small opening on the back edge. Turn wing right side out. Make the second wing the same way. Lay wings against the side of the owlett and ladderstitch in place following the guide line on the pattern. (See Fig. d).

6 Finish by grooming all the seams carefully to release any pile trapped in the stitching. Brush face mask away from each eye.

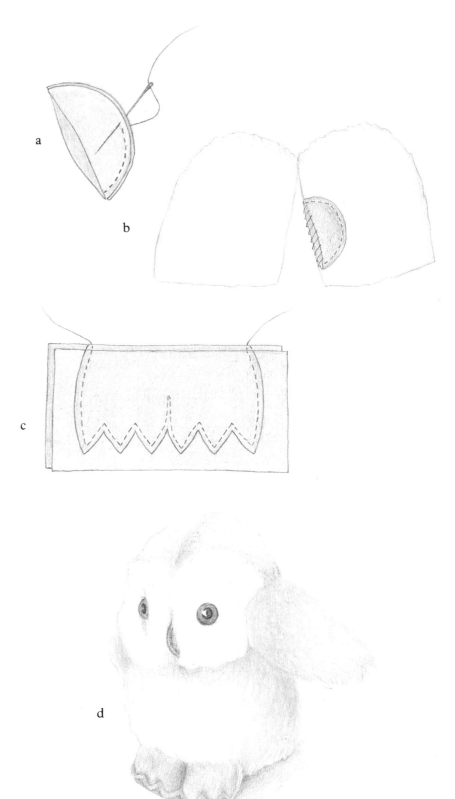

a

b

c

d

LITTLE BLUE

MATERIALS NEEDED

46 cm (18 in) square of short pile
polished blue fur
46 cm (18 in) square of short pile
unpolished white fur
30.5 cm (12 in) square grey
needlecord
227 g (8 oz) stuffing
A pair of 16 mm blue safety eyes
Black embroidery thread

Height of Penguin 28 cm (11 in)

*This is the smallest of all the penguins and is to be found
living in the coastal waters of southern Australia and New
Zealand. The upright stance of the penguin on land is
because the short legs are set far back on the body. This of
course results in the endearing waddle so characteristic of
these birds.*

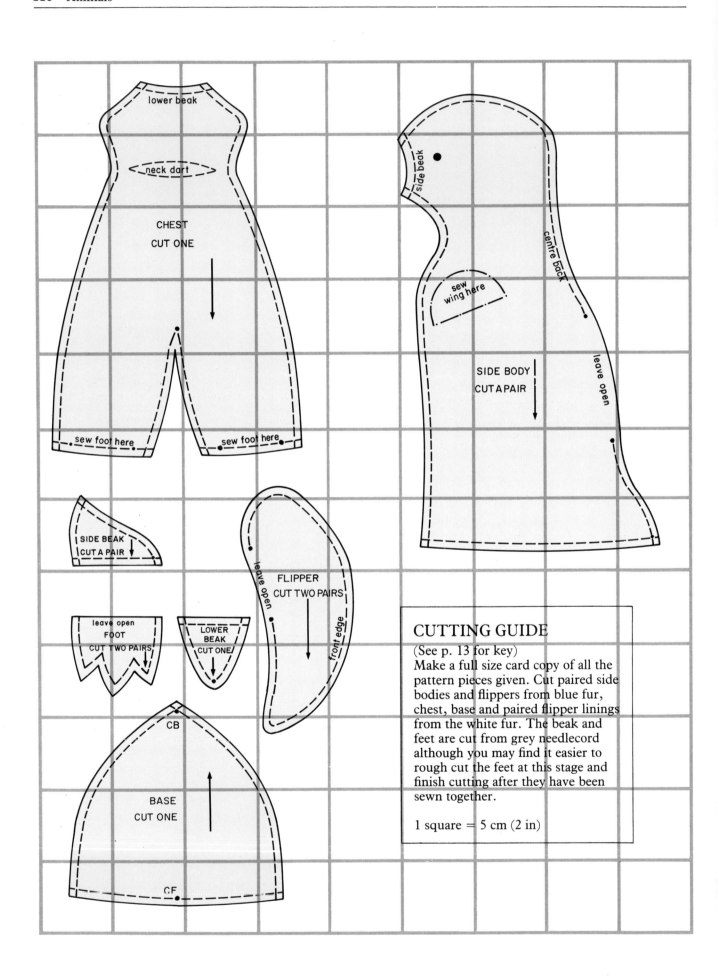

lower beak

neck dart

CHEST
CUT ONE

sew foot here   sew foot here

SIDE BEAK
CUT A PAIR

leave open
FOOT
CUT TWO PAIRS

LOWER
BEAK
CUT ONE

leave open

FLIPPER
CUT TWO PAIRS

front edge

CB

BASE
CUT ONE

CF

side beak

sew
wing here

centre back

SIDE BODY
CUT A PAIR

leave open

CUTTING GUIDE

(See p. 13 for key)
Make a full size card copy of all the
pattern pieces given. Cut paired side
bodies and flippers from blue fur,
chest, base and paired flipper linings
from the white fur. The beak and
feet are cut from grey needlecord
although you may find it easier to
rough cut the feet at this stage and
finish cutting after they have been
sewn together.

1 square = 5 cm (2 in)

1 Sew an upper beak to each corresponding side body and the lower beak to the chest. Place side bodies right sides together and sew from the top of the beak round the head and down the back to the base. Remember to leave an opening in the lower back for turning skin through.

2 Make the neck dart in the chest then the dart at the lower centre front between the feet. This will round out the body. Fit the completed chest between the side bodies and sew from the tip of the beak down the base on each side in turn. Take care to fit the curves of the neck together without making the head twist.

3 Sew each foot together around the edge and finish cutting out if necessary. Clip between the toes. Turn feet right side out and topstitch down between the toes. Stuff each toe then the feet and baste straight edge of feet to the lower edge of the chest with all raw edges level. Sew after checking that feet are centred correctly. (See Fig. a).

4 Fit base in place and sew, making sure that the feet are securely held. Turn completed skin right side out and fix eyes in place. Stuff the beak, head and body firmly. Check that the Penguin sits level on the table before closing the opening with ladder stitch.

5 Sew a blue and white flipper together round the edge leaving a small opening. Turn right side out and close the opening. Ladderstitch flipper to side of body with lining on the inside. Make and attach the second flipper in the same way to the other side of the body.

6 Work straight stitch nostrils high on the beak using all six strands of black embroidery thread. Work stitches together, pulling from side to side to narrow the beak and give more shaping. (See Fig. b). Groom your Little Blue, releasing any fur pile trapped in the seams.

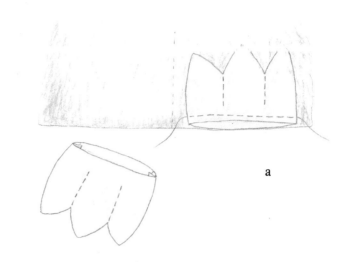

a

b

GILBERT THE GIBBON

MATERIALS NEEDED

45.5 cm × 137 cm (18 in × 54 in) long pile blond fur

45.5 cm (18 in) square of flesh coloured short pile, unpolished fur

625 g (1 lb 6 oz) stuffing

A pair of 16 mm brown safety eyes

Brown embroidery thread

Height of Gibbon 61 cm (24 in)

Gibbons are Asiatic apes noted for the skill with which they swing through the forest canopy. They move with such speed and agility that it is quite breathtaking to behold. Choose a very long pile fur for the body and a light colour, short pile fur or even velvet for the face as dark-faced apes can be frightening to young children.

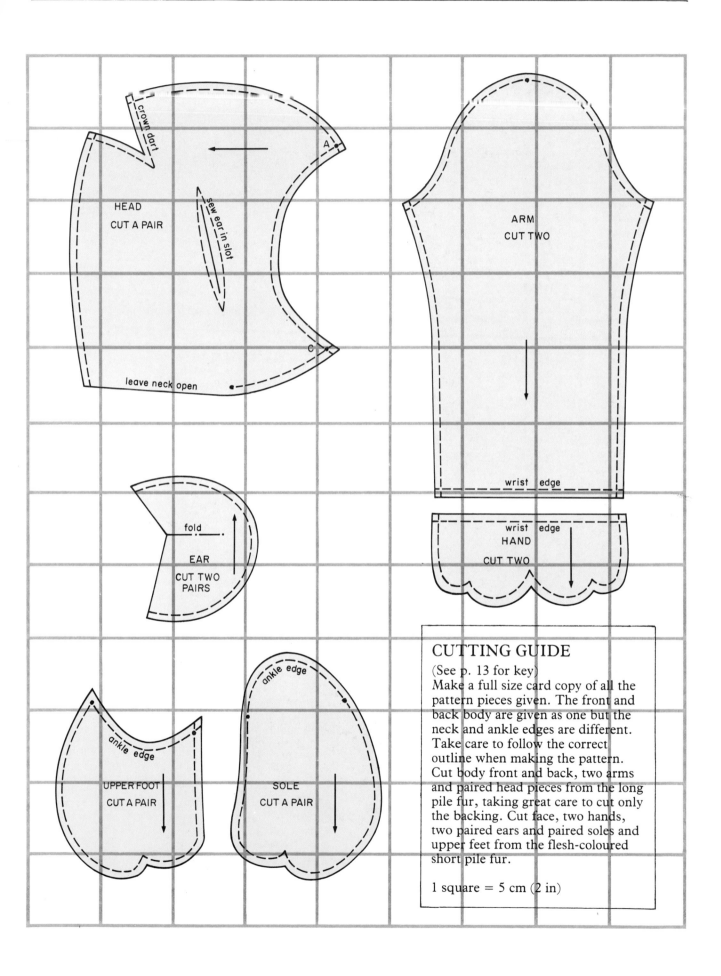

HEAD
CUT A PAIR

crown dart

sew ear in slot

leave neck open

A

C

ARM
CUT TWO

wrist edge

wrist edge
HAND
CUT TWO

fold

EAR

CUT TWO
PAIRS

ankle edge

UPPER FOOT
CUT A PAIR

ankle edge

SOLE
CUT A PAIR

CUTTING GUIDE
(See p. 13 for key)
Make a full size card copy of all the
pattern pieces given. The front and
back body are given as one but the
neck and ankle edges are different.
Take care to follow the correct
outline when making the pattern.
Cut body front and back, two arms
and paired head pieces from the long
pile fur, taking great care to cut only
the backing. Cut face, two hands,
two paired ears and paired soles and
upper feet from the flesh-coloured
short pile fur.

1 square = 5 cm (2 in)

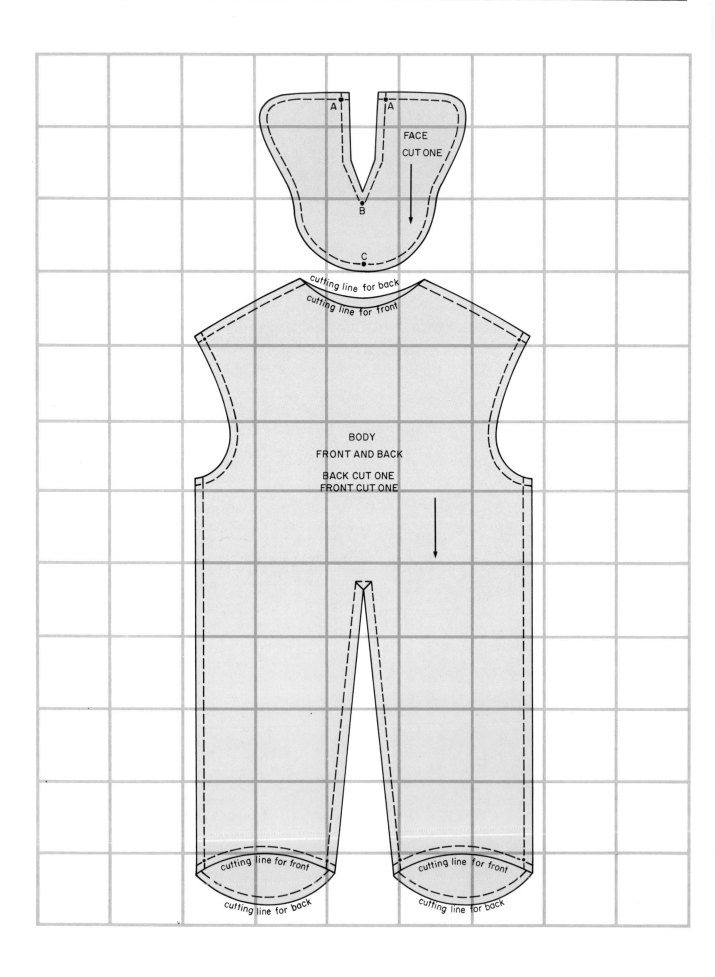

FACE
CUT ONE

A A

B

C

cutting line for back
cutting line for front

BODY
FRONT AND BACK

BACK CUT ONE
FRONT CUT ONE

cutting line for front
cutting line for back

cutting line for front
cutting line for back

MAKING THE HEAD

1 Take a pair of ear pieces and sew them together round the outer curved edge then turn right side out. Fold the top down till all straight edges lie together then oversew to hold the fold in place. Fit completed ear in matching slot on side of head with fold lying towards the face. Sew in place securely. Make the second ear in the same way but fold to the opposite side and sew in place.

2 Sew the crown darts on each side of the head then sew heads together along the centre back from the forehead at A down to the neck edge. Sew the under chin seam from C down to the neck edge.

3 Fold face mask to bring both As together then sew the centre front dart from A to B. Fit face into opening on front of head, match A to A and C to C. Baste in place, easing in fullness around the chin then sew. (See Fig. a).

4 Turn completed head skin right side out and fix safety eyes in place in required position. You must decide for yourself where you want to put the eyes in response to the colour of fur being used.

5 Stuff head firmly, rounding out the cheeks and especially the jaw. Gather up neck edge slightly and work straight stitches across the opening to hold the stuffing in place. Use all six strands of embroidery thread to work two straight stitch nostrils. (See Fig. b). Set head aside.

a
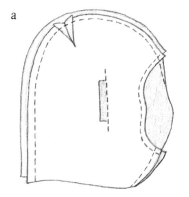

MAKING THE BODY

6 Sew an upper foot to each front ankle edge and a sole to each back ankle edge. Check that big toes are on the inside. Sew front and back body together at shoulders.

7 Sew a hand to the wrist edge of an arm then fit the arm into the side of the body matching up head of arm with the shoulder seam and sew in place. Fold arm in half lengthways and sew hand, underarm and body side seams continuously. Work other side in the same way.

8 Sew inside leg seam on each side in turn from the top down to the ankle. Ease upper foot to fit sole then seam from ankle edge, side to side. (See Fig. c). Sew second foot in the same way.

9 Turn body skin right side out through the neck, be careful not to overstretch the opening. Stuff body lightly and leave shoulders somewhat empty so that the arms can move freely. Draw up neck edge and work straight stitches across opening to hold stuffing in place. Ladderstitch head to body and finally groom Gilbert with a good, stiff brushing.

b

c
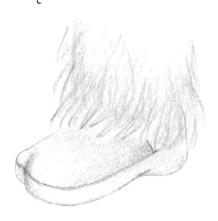

SELINA SEAL

Selina is delightfully easy to make and is a most appealing soft toy with her lovely soft, silky white coat and large blue eyes. The whiskers are made from loops of invisible sewing thread which are sewn securely in place. However, these are probably best omitted if the toy is destined for a very young child.

MATERIALS NEEDED
61 cm × 137 cm (24 in × 54 in)
   medium pile white fur
227 g (8 oz) stuffing
A pair of 18 mm blue safety eyes
Nylon invisible sewing thread
Black embroidery thread

Length of Seal 40 cm (16 in)
Height of Seal 25 cm (10 in)

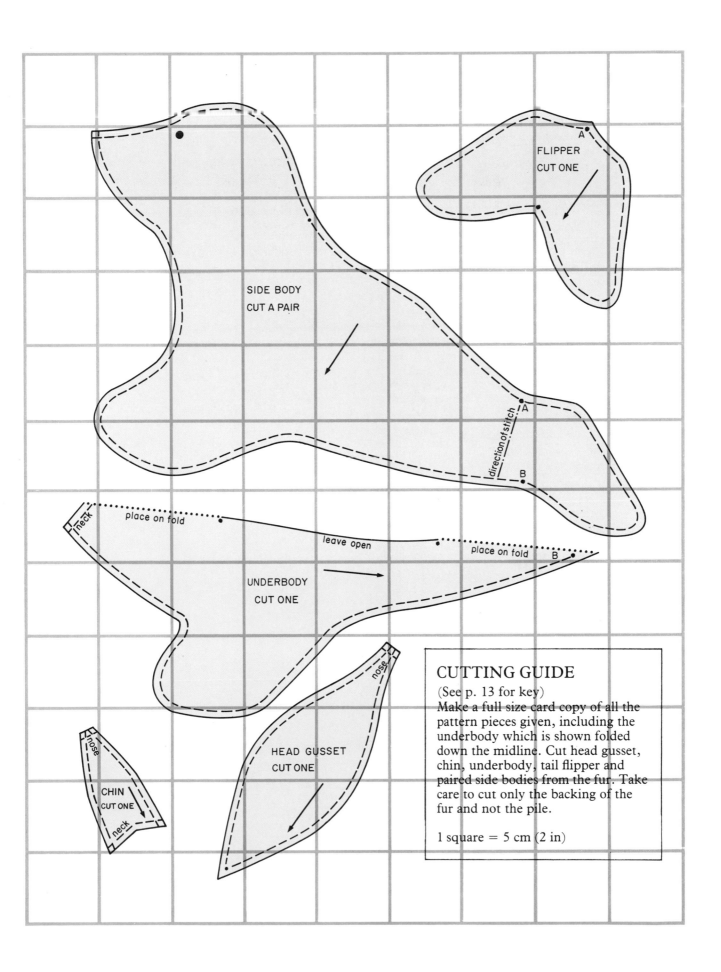

FLIPPER
CUT ONE

A

SIDE BODY
CUT A PAIR

direction of stitch

A

B

neck

place on fold

leave open

place on fold

B

UNDERBODY

CUT ONE

nose

nose

CHIN
CUT ONE

HEAD GUSSET
CUT ONE

neck

CUTTING GUIDE
(See p. 13 for key)
Make a full size card copy of all the
pattern pieces given, including the
underbody which is shown folded
down the midline. Cut head gusset,
chin, underbody, tail flipper and
paired side bodies from the fur. Take
care to cut only the backing of the
fur and not the pile.

1 square = 5 cm (2 in)

1 Sew chin and underbody together along the neck edge. Fit the completed underbody gusset between each side body starting at the front and working back to the match point B by the flippers. Sew each side in turn.

2 Now fit the head gusset between the side bodies again working from the nose at the front to the match point at the back of the head. When satisfied with the fit, sew the gusset in place. Finish sewing the side bodies together along the top back down to A. Close the short nose seam between the head gusset and the chin.

3 Spread open the body flippers and fit the separate flipper section in place. Line up match points at A and B then sew all round taking care to tuck the pile in and not trap it in the seams. Turn completed skin right side out through central opening in underbody.
(See Fig. a).

4 Check all seams then insert safety eyes. Stuff the body firmly except for the flippers which should be left as empty flaps. Close the opening with ladder stitch. Stitch the flippers open by taking a stitch down from A through the body to the base and pulling up fairly tight before fastening off. (See Fig. b).

5 Work a block of satin stitches for the nose using all six strands of the embroidery thread and a straight stitch mouth caught down in the middle.

6 The whiskers are made by using doubled invisible thread in the needle and working large loops which are backstitched in place at the base. Work two or three tiny back stitches to hold each loop and then tug the loop to check that it is secure. The back stitches will be quite invisible down in the pile. Work several loops on each side of the nose then cut and trim them to the required length. (See Fig. c).

a

b

c

BESHIUNG-CHIN

The giant Panda lives in the mountainous regions of Szechuan and Yunnan, provinces of China that border on to Tibet. The local name for the Panda is Beshiung-chin which means white bear. It is one of the world's rarest and most puzzling animals virtually unknown outside China before 1869 when a French zoologist Père Armand David first saw some pelts and came to suspect its existence.

MATERIALS NEEDED

30.5 cm × 137 cm (12 in × 54 in)
  wide black fur
30.5 cm × 137 cm (12 in × 54 in)
  wide off-white fur
454 g (1 lb) stuffing
A pair of 18 mm brown safety eyes
Black embroidery thread

Height of Panda 24 cm (9½ in)
Length of Panda 40 cm (16 in)

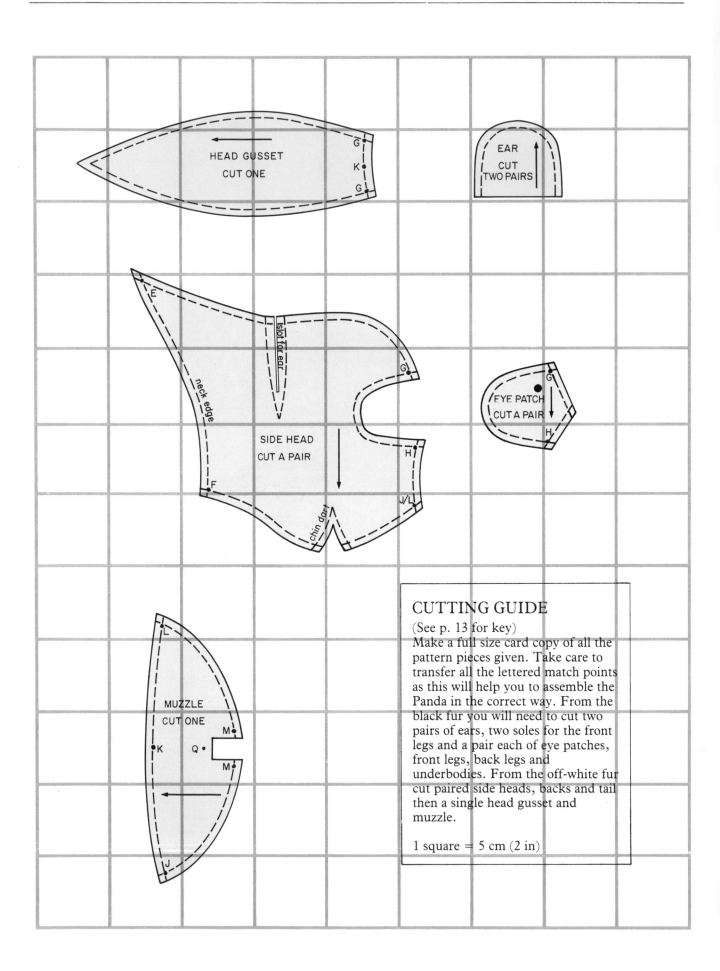

HEAD GUSSET
CUT ONE

EAR
CUT
TWO PAIRS

slot for ear

neck edge

SIDE HEAD
CUT A PAIR

chin dart

EYE PATCH
CUT A PAIR

MUZZLE
CUT ONE

CUTTING GUIDE

(See p. 13 for key)

Make a full size card copy of all the pattern pieces given. Take care to transfer all the lettered match points as this will help you to assemble the Panda in the correct way. From the black fur you will need to cut two pairs of ears, two soles for the front legs and a pair each of eye patches, front legs, back legs and underbodies. From the off-white fur cut paired side heads, backs and tail then a single head gusset and muzzle.

1 square = 5 cm (2 in)

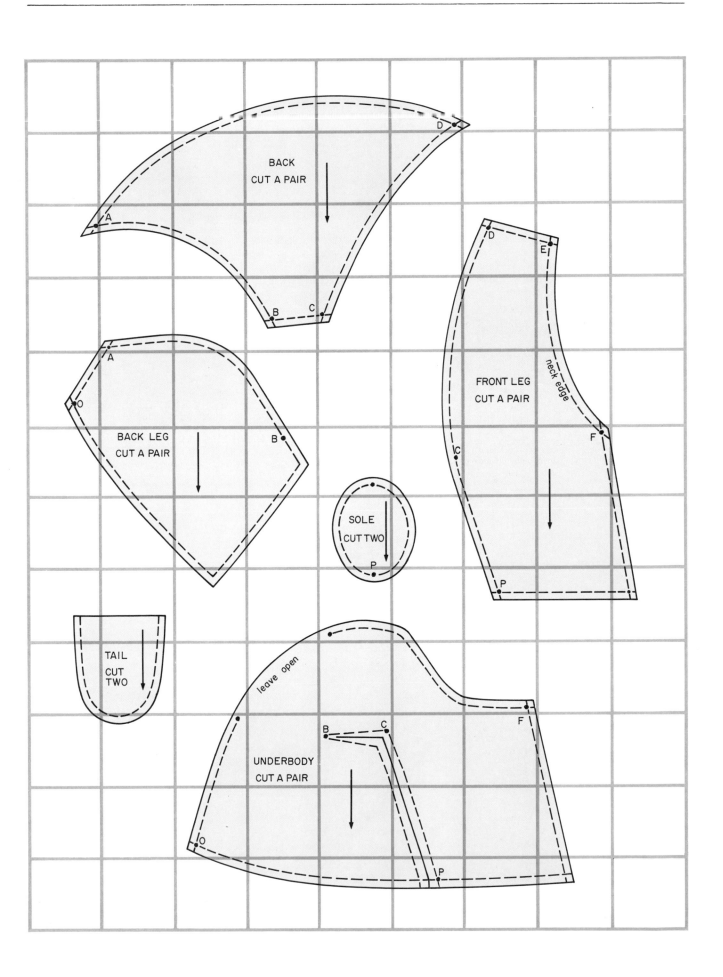

BACK
CUT A PAIR

D

A

B   C

BACK LEG
CUT A PAIR

A

O

B

FRONT LEG
CUT A PAIR

D   E

neck edge

C

F

P

SOLE
CUT TWO

P

TAIL
CUT
TWO

UNDERBODY
CUT A PAIR

leave open

B   C

F

O

P

MAKING THE BODY

1 Start by sewing the various black and white sections together to complete paired side bodies. The back legs are sewn to the back from A to B and the front legs are sewn to the back from D to C. (See Fig. a).

2 Now sew complete side bodies together from the neck at E back to O, this makes the centre back seam. Sew underbodies together from O to F, leaving a central opening for stuffing.

3 Open underbody out and position against each side matching up the legs and with right sides together sew from O around back leg through B–C to P at heel of the front leg on each side in turn. Sew each front leg front seam from toes up to F. Set body aside. (See Fig. b).

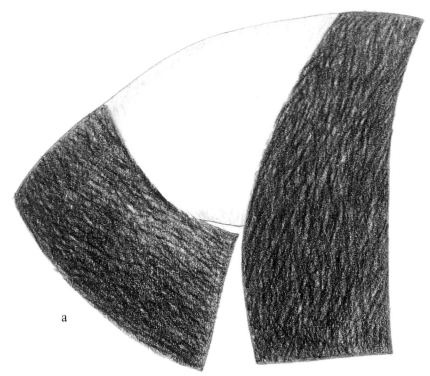

a

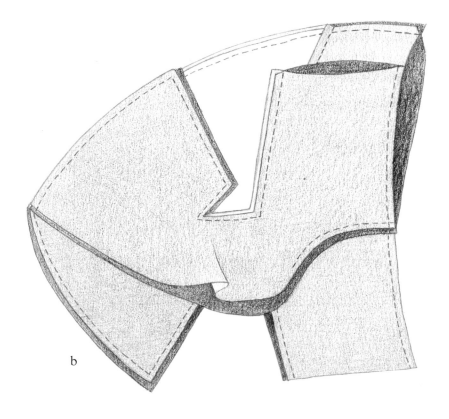

b

MAKING THE HEAD

4 Work a row of stay stitch around the curve of the eye patch edge on the side head from G to H. Clip into the stay stitch to release the tension then fit matching eye patch in place and pin at right angles to the edge. Backstitch patch in place. Work second eye patch in the same way. (See Fig. c).

5 Make the ears by sewing together in pairs around the curved edges. Turn tight side out and sew an ear in each slot on the sides of the head. Sew head gusset in place by sewing from G back towards E on each side in turn. Sew remaining short section beyond head gusset to E. (See Fig. d).

6 Open out head and match muzzle in place and sew from J through K to L on the other side. Sew both small chin darts then refold head bringing Ms together and J and L together. Sew from M at tip of muzzle back through J–L to F. Press nose flat to match M to Q. Sew across the snout.

7 Turn completed head right side out and check all seams before proceeding. When happy with the appearance, fix the safety eyes in place. Now turn head around and push nose first through the neck opening of the body. Match up E and F of head to E and F of body then sew the two together.

8 Turn completed skin right side out through the opening in the underbody. Stuff the head first followed by the front legs, back legs and body generally. Ladderstitch opening.

9 Sew tail pieces together round curved edge. Turn right side out and tuck in raw edges. Oversew edges together then ladderstitch tail to back of body.

10 Embroider a block of satin stitch for the nose and a straight stitch mouth caught down in the middle. (See Fig. e).

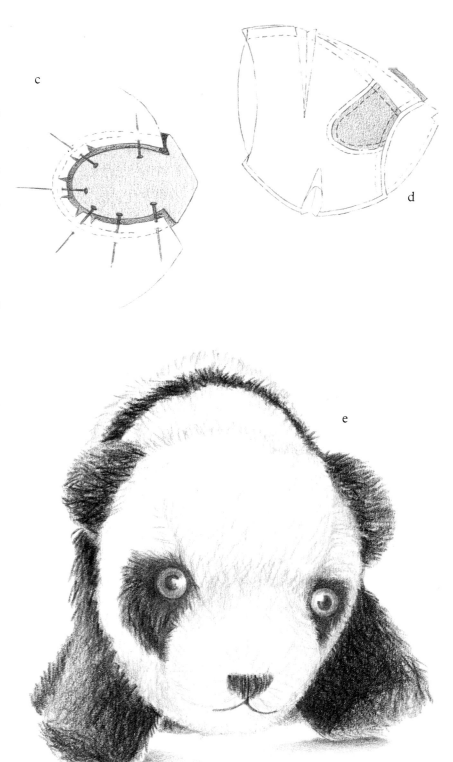

c

d

e

DORINDA DRAGON

This most gentle of dragons is a real delight. Making her in velvet is undoubtedly a challenge and will require all your skills and patience. A simpler solution if you can't resist the challenge would be to make her in fine wool or needlecord.

MATERIALS NEEDED

1 m × 92 cm (36 in × 36 in) wide red
  cotton velvet
15 cm (6 in) square of yellow cotton
46 cm × 15 cm (18 in × 6 in) wide
  polyester batting
454 g (1 lb) stuffing
A pair of 18 mm safety eyes with lids
  and eyelashes
Approximately 12 gold sequins and
  small beads
Golden yellow embroidery thread

Height of Dragon 35 cm (14 in)
Length of Dragon 35 cm (14 in)

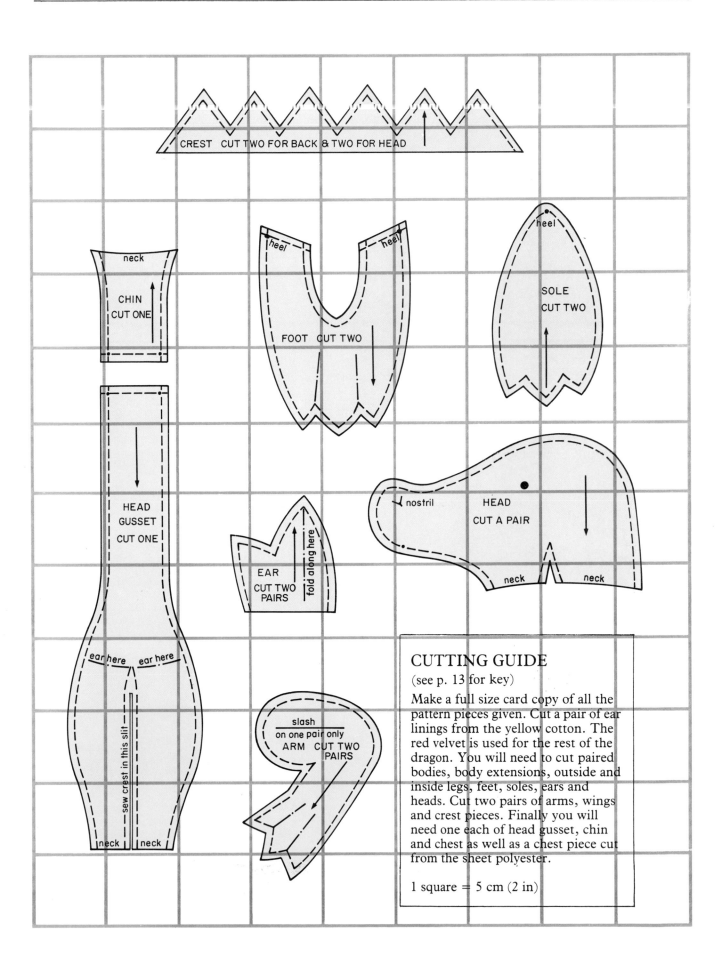

CREST CUT TWO FOR BACK & TWO FOR HEAD

neck

CHIN
CUT ONE

heel   heel

FOOT CUT TWO

heel

SOLE
CUT TWO

HEAD
GUSSET
CUT ONE

fold along here

EAR
CUT TWO
PAIRS

nostril   HEAD
CUT A PAIR

neck   neck

ear here   ear here

sew crest in this slit

neck   neck

slash
on one pair only
ARM CUT TWO
PAIRS

CUTTING GUIDE
(see p. 13 for key)

Make a full size card copy of all the
pattern pieces given. Cut a pair of ear
linings from the yellow cotton. The
red velvet is used for the rest of the
dragon. You will need to cut paired
bodies, body extensions, outside and
inside legs, feet, soles, ears and
heads. Cut two pairs of arms, wings
and crest pieces. Finally you will
need one each of head gusset, chin
and chest as well as a chest piece cut
from the sheet polyester.

1 square = 5 cm (2 in)

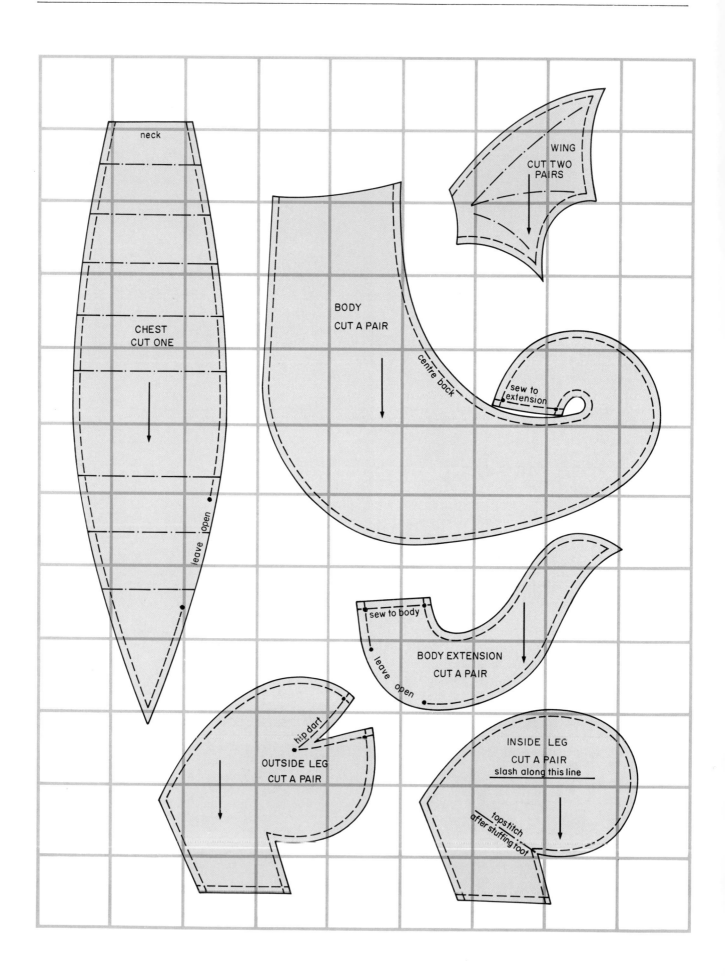

MAKING THE BODY

1 Take a pair of crest pieces and sew them together down the jaggered edge. Trim seam allowance, clip between the spines and then turn right side out. Baste edges together then with all raw edges level sew the crest to the back of one body piece. (See Fig. a).

2 Sew a body extension to each body in turn then sew them together down the centre back from the neck to the tip of the tail taking care that they don't slip when sewing the tight inside curve of the tail.

3 Sew velvet chest to sheet polyester chest piece all round the edge then machine quilt into sections by topstitching along the guide lines marked on the pattern. Fit chest between body and sew down from neck edge to tip on each side in turn, leaving an opening on one side only. Finish sewing body together by completing the under tail seam again leaving the opening marked on the pattern.

4 There is an art in turning the body skin right side out and it is simply to do it in two stages. Turn the tip of the tail out through the tail opening then feed it back into the same opening and out through the chest opening. Turn remainder of body right side out either through the chest or the neck. Check that all the seams are secure and that there has been no slippage.

5 Stuff the tip of the tail and close the tail opening. Stuff remainder of the tail through the chest and then stuff the body proper, moulding out a good, rounded shape and twisting the tail into a pleasing position. Close chest and draw up the neck edge just sufficient to roll the raw edges over. Hold stuffing in place with a grid of straight stitches worked across the neck from side to side.

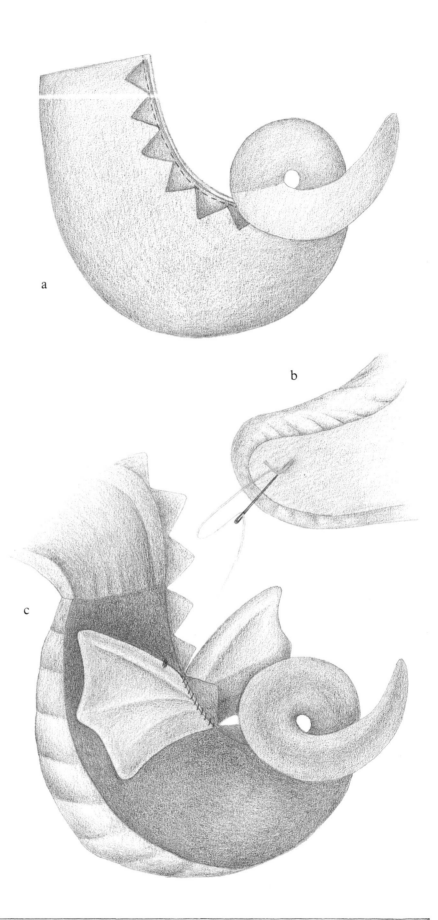

a

b

c

MAKING THE HEAD

6 Take the second pair of crest pieces and sew them together and prepare as already described. Cut them in half and use three spines to sew in the neck end of the head gusset. Discard the remaining three spines.

7 Sew chin to head gusset across short end then fit gusset strip between head pieces from neck at front, round head to neck at back. Sew each side in turn carefully, especially round the curve of the nostrils.

8 Make neck darts in each head piece. Then turn head right side out and fix eyes in place. Stuff head firmly. Gather edge and draw up just sufficiently to roll raw edges inwards. Hold stuffing in place by working straight stitches across the neck. Now ladderstitch the head to the body.

9 Sew a lining to each ear, turn right side out tucking in the base and folding as directed on the pattern. Oversew edges together to hold the folds then ladderstitch each ear in place on the head.

10 Embroider nostrils by working a fly stitch on each side of the snout. Decorate the forehead with scattered sequins stitched in place with small beads, alternatively embroider golden yellow French knots. (See Fig. b).

MAKING THE WINGS

11 Sew a pair of wing pieces together, trim seam allowance and turn right side out. Topstitch the three divisions then stuff the upper and lower channels. This will provide the wing with some firmness. Turn in edges at the base and oversew them together. Now sew wing in place on the back through the third spine down from the neck. This is easier to do than it sounds. Make second wing in the same way and sew to the other side of the spine. Catch top edges of both wings down on to the body about 2.5 cm (1 in) out from the spines. (See Fig. c).

MAKING THE LIMBS

12 Sew a pair of arm pieces together all round the edge then turn right side out through the slash. Topstitch finger divisions then stuff arm firmly. Close slash with herringbone stitch and ladderstitch arm on side of body approximately level with the third chest division and in line with the wings. Make the second arm in the same way and sew to the other side of the body.

13 Make the dart in the outside leg then sew a pair of leg pieces together up the front edge. Open out and sew the foot to the ankle edge. Refold foot to bring back edges together and sew from the heel upwards and around the leg to meet the seaming on the front. Fit and sew sole in place.

14 Turn leg right side out through the slash. Topstitch between each of the toes then stuff the foot and lower leg firmly. Now topstitch in from the back edge of the leg up towards the knee. Continue stuffing the leg, filling out the haunch. Close slash with herringbone stitch. (See Fig. d).

d

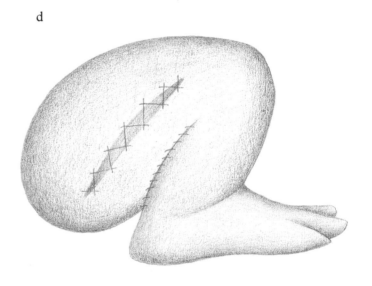

15 Push leg together to bring back edges side by side then ladderstitch them together. Place leg against matching side of body and make second leg at this stage. Move legs around to find the position that enables your dragon to stand. The shoulders and hips will usually line up under the neck darts in the head. Ladderstitch legs in place securely.

BUMBLES THE BEAR

*Big brown bears are found throughout the northern
hemisphere and, surprisingly perhaps to some, there are
scattered populations in France, Italy and Spain.
They are known regionally by a variety of names such as the
Kodiak bear and Grizzly. These bears vary in colour from
pale yellowish-fawn to a dark brown that is almost
black. Bears are large, immensely powerful carnivores and
either live alone or in family groups.*

MATERIALS NEEDED

46 cm × 137 cm (18 in × 54 in) wide
   short pile dark brown fur
23 cm (9 in) square of brown velour
340 g (12 oz) stuffing
A pair of 18 mm amber safety eyes
Black embroidery thread
1 m (1 yard) yellow ribbon

Height of Bear 33 cm (13 in)

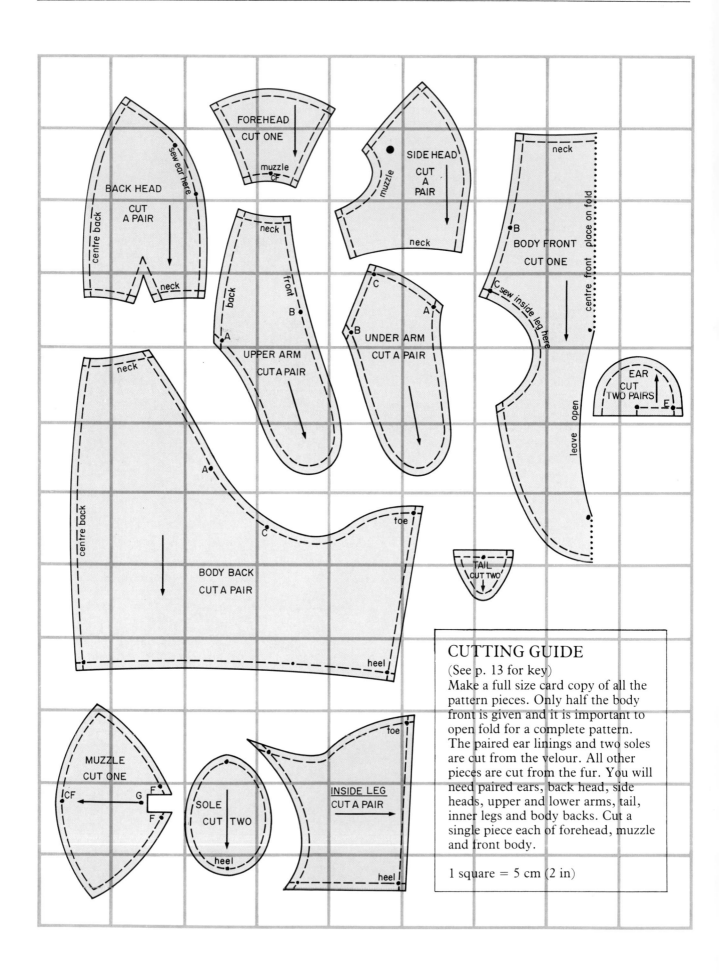

FOREHEAD
CUT ONE

muzzle
CF

BACK HEAD
CUT
A PAIR

sew ear here

centre back

neck

SIDE HEAD
CUT
A
PAIR

muzzle

neck

neck

B

BODY FRONT
CUT ONE

place on fold

centre front

C sew inside leg here

leave open

neck

back

front

B

A

UPPER ARM
CUT A PAIR

C

A

B

UNDER ARM
CUT A PAIR

EAR
CUT
TWO PAIRS

E

neck

centre back

A

C

toe

BODY BACK

CUT A PAIR

heel

TAIL
CUT TWO

MUZZLE
CUT ONE

CF

G

F

F

SOLE
CUT TWO

heel

toe

INSIDE LEG
CUT A PAIR

heel

CUTTING GUIDE
(See p. 13 for key)
Make a full size card copy of all the pattern pieces. Only half the body front is given and it is important to open fold for a complete pattern. The paired ear linings and two soles are cut from the velour. All other pieces are cut from the fur. You will need paired ears, back head, side heads, upper and lower arms, tail, inner legs and body backs. Cut a single piece each of forehead, muzzle and front body.

1 square = 5 cm (2 in)

MAKING THE BODY

1 Sew upper arms to body front from the neck edge down to the Bs. Now sew underarms to upper arms around paws from A to B. Stitch upper arms in turn to body backs from neck edge down to As. Sew the pointed flaps of the underarms to the body front from B to C and to the body backs from A to C. (See Fig. a).

2 Sew an inside leg to body front on each side in turn then sew inside legs to body backs along the top edge from C down to toes. (See Fig. b).

3 Sew the centre back seam from neck to base. Sew tail pieces togethr and turn right side out. Sew tail to bottom of centre back seam with raw edges level.

4 Continue sewing legs together on each side in turn by sewing back from heels to match points on bottom edge. Fit soles in place and baste, then sew. Turn to the right side and check that they arc satisfactory before continuing. Finish sewing front to back body by sewing along bottom edges lining up centre front with centre back seam under the tail. Set body aside.

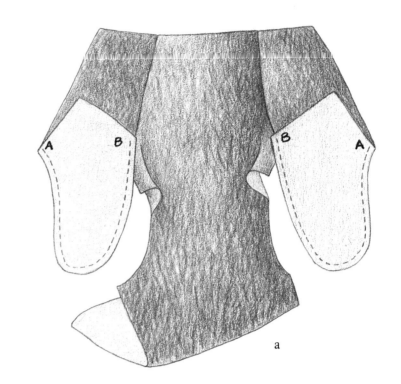

a

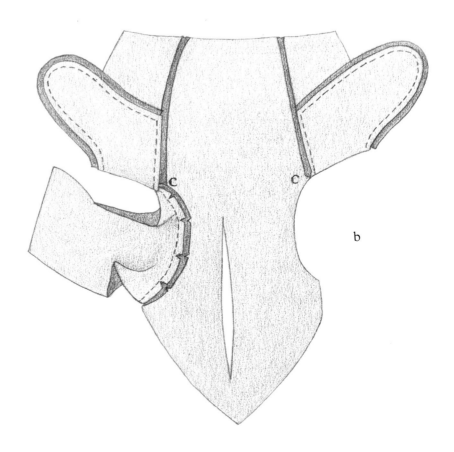

b

MAKING THE HEAD

5 Sew a lining on each ear then turn them right side out. Tuck in seam allowance at the base of each ear between slit and outer curve at E and oversew edges together. Position raw edge of ears against side seams of back head pieces and sew in place. Sew darts on neck edge then sew back heads together down the centre back. (See Fig. c).

6 Sew side heads to either side of forehead. Position muzzle matching centres then sew from side to side. Refold front of head to bring edges of muzzle together and sew from snout at F down to the neck edge. Press snout flat to bring F and G together and sew.

7 Open out front head and sew to back head taking care not to trap the upper edges of each ear. Turn head right side out and fix eyes in place. Now push head down through neck opening of body and line up centre front and back seams. Sew in place either backstitching by hand with strong thread or by machine. Use whichever method you feel most comfortable with.

8 Turn the completed skin right side out through the slit in the lower body front. Check all seams at this point for strength before continuing. Stuff muzzle first followed by the head. Use the neck seam to hold stuffing in place. Now stuff legs, arms upper body and lastly the lower body. Ladderstitch opening. Mould body by hand, gently pulling in arms to rest in lap.

9 Ladderstitch ears into a pleasing curve on the side heads then embroider a satin stitch nose and straight stitch mouth. Finish Bumbles by tying a bow around the neck.

c

DRESSED ANIMALS

Many of the most popular stories written for children feature animals dressed as people. These animals are frequently endowed with human characteristics and the most endearing personalities. Walt Disney, Beatrix Potter and Joel Harris all recognized this appeal and put it to good use. Dressed animals as toys are just as appealing as their literary cousins, for youngsters will often regard these characters as personal friends and confidants, forming long-lasting attachments with them.

This collection of patterns consists of a few basic bodies that are used to make several different characters and by enlarging or reducing these patterns you will be able to extend the range to make families. The clutch body used for Ken Kitten and Abeargail is designed for the very young, the clothes being few and simple. Edward and Edwina, on the other hand, have an age-less appeal, Teddies being the most popular of all soft toys ever designed. They are dressed in Edwardian sailor suits as befits their names. Melissa Mouse, Harriet Hare and Brock the Badger are for older children who will find much pleasure in dressing these toys with their special outfits which are cleverly adapted for tails and ears.

① A Couple of Kittens
② Abeargail
③ Edward and Edwina
④ Melissa Mouse
⑤ Harriet Hare
⑥ Brock the Badger

A COUPLE OF KITTENS

The cat family has an amazing variety of coat colours, patterns and lengths. By choosing the furs carefully you will be able to use this basic kitten pattern to make any number of striped and spotted jungle cats as well as tabbies, Persians, plain coloured moggies and the lovable twosome shown here.

MATERIALS NEEDED FOR KEN KITTEN

50 cm × 68 cm (18 in × 27 in) wide white fur
227 g (8 oz) stuffing
A pair of 16 mm blue safety eyes
Embroidery thread for nose

MATERIALS NEEDED FOR OLIVER OCELOT

50 cm × 68 cm wide (18 in × 27 in) wide spotted fur
227 g (8 oz) stuffing
A pair of 18 mm yellow safety eyes with slit pupil
Black safety nose

Height of each Animal 29 cm (11 in)

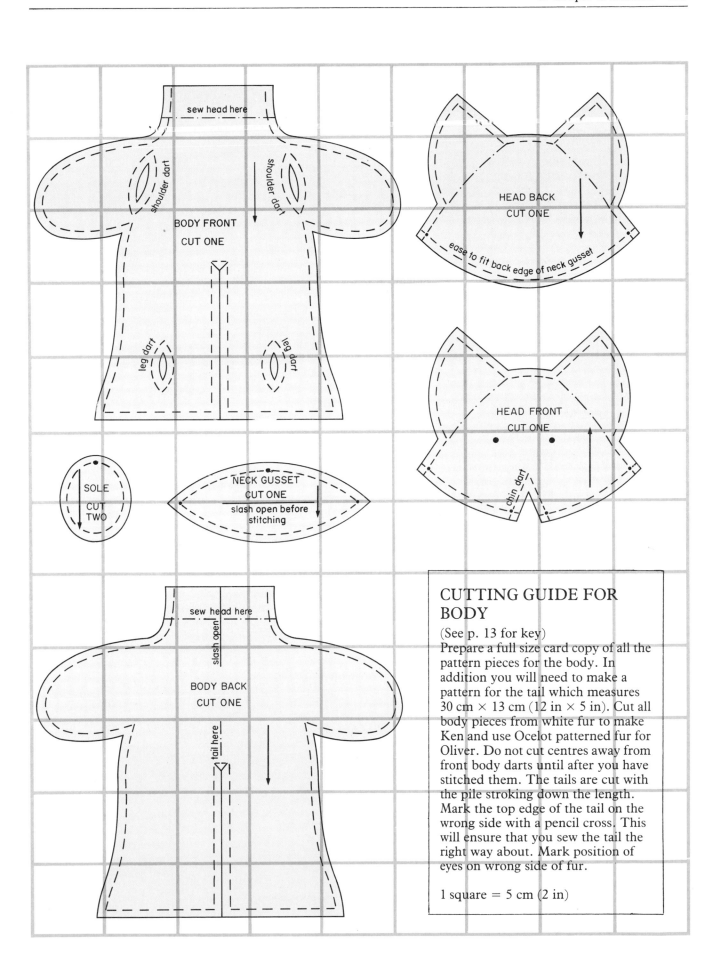

sew head here

shoulder dart

shoulder dart

BODY FRONT
CUT ONE

leg dart

leg dart

HEAD BACK
CUT ONE

ease to fit back edge of neck gusset

HEAD FRONT
CUT ONE

chin dart

SOLE
CUT
TWO

NECK GUSSET
CUT ONE
slash open before
stitching

sew head here

slash open

BODY BACK
CUT ONE

tail here

CUTTING GUIDE FOR BODY

(See p. 13 for key)
Prepare a full size card copy of all the pattern pieces for the body. In addition you will need to make a pattern for the tail which measures 30 cm × 13 cm (12 in × 5 in). Cut all body pieces from white fur to make Ken and use Ocelot patterned fur for Oliver. Do not cut centres away from front body darts until after you have stitched them. The tails are cut with the pile stroking down the length. Mark the top edge of the tail on the wrong side with a pencil cross. This will ensure that you sew the tail the right way about. Mark position of eyes on wrong side of fur.

1 square = 5 cm (2 in)

MAKING THE BODY

1 Working on one side of the front body at a time, fold an arm and leg inwards and sew the shoulder and leg darts. Repeat with the limbs on the other side. These darts bring the limbs forward. Trim darts to release tension or cut centres away. (See Fig. a).

2 Work a row of stay stitching down each side of the neck slit on the back, then place front and back bodies together and sew the outline leaving lower edges, neck and neck slit open. Clip corners. Position the soles with the match points to the front, press the leg side seams open and baste first before sewing.

3 Turn completed body skin right side out and stuff limbs first followed by tummy and chest. Close slit opening on back and fill neck to overflowing. Run a gathering thread around top of neck and pull up. Run a second row of gathering along the placement line marked for the head. This results in a firm neck stump. Clean seams and set body aside. Then fold head front in half and sew the chin dart. (See Fig. b).

4 Sew head front and back pieces together, leaving lower curved edge open. (See Fig. c). Work a row of stay stitching along each side of the slash in the neck gusset.

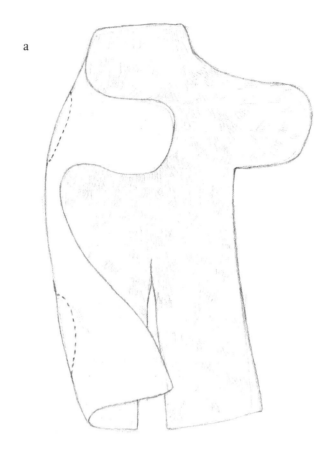

a

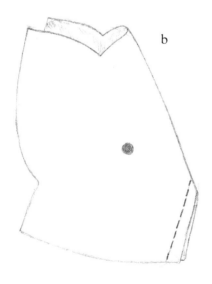

b

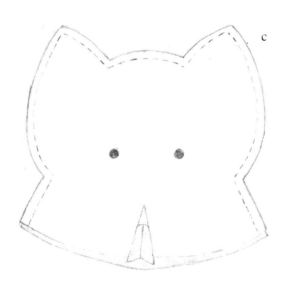

c

5 Position gusset between front and back with match points to side and front. Sew in place, gently easing fullness along back edge. (See Fig. d). Turn head right side out through gusset opening. Insert safety eyes now, checking that slit pupils are correctly aligned. Also insert safety nose for Oliver Ocelot at this stage.

6 Topstitch base of each ear then fill head with stuffing fibre, rounding out the cheeks and chin. Make a cavity in the stuffing with two fingers. This should be just large enough to fit the neck stump on the body. Lower head on to body with a twisting movement until happy with the appearance. Ladderstitch in position along the placement line. Embroider a satin stitch nose and straight stitch mouth for Ken Kitten.

7 Fold tail in half lengthways and, with fur stroking down, sew lower short edge and the length. Turn right side out. Hold tail in left hand with seam under thumb, bring sides together and ladderstitch to enclose seam. Pull up on stitches to make tail curl. This method of making a tail results in four thicknesses of fur and eliminates the need for any stuffing. Ladderstitch tail in place on back of body. (See Fig. e).

d

e

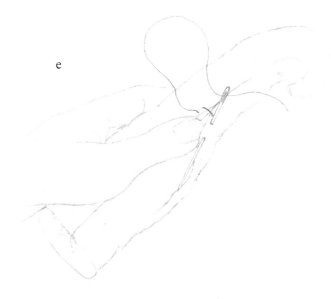

DUNGAREES

**MATERIALS NEEDED
FOR DUNGAREES**
23 cm × 115 cm wide (9 in × 45 in)
   wide jersey
2 buttons
2 snaps
Hook and eye

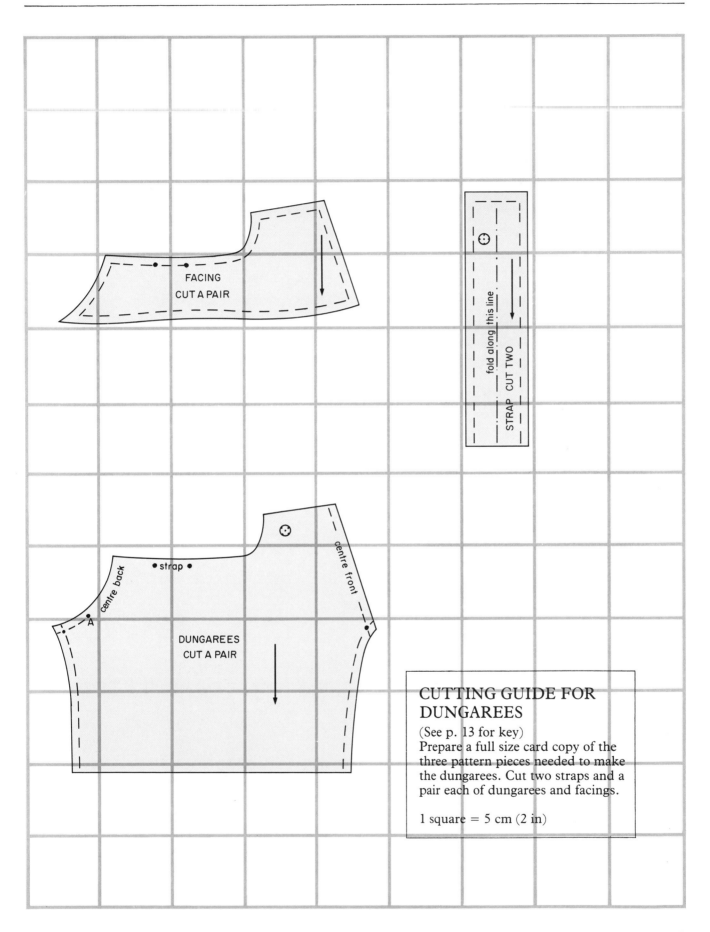

FACING
CUT A PAIR

fold along this line
STRAP CUT TWO

centre back
• strap •
centre front
A
DUNGAREES
CUT A PAIR

CUTTING GUIDE FOR DUNGAREES
(See p. 13 for key)
Prepare a full size card copy of the three pattern pieces needed to make the dungarees. Cut two straps and a pair each of dungarees and facings.

1 square = 5 cm (2 in)

MAKING THE DUNGAREES

1 Sew facings right sides together at centre front. Press seam open and neaten lower edge. (See Fig. a). Fold strap in half and sew down the length and across the short end. Trim seam, cut corners off and turn right side out. Press, then topstitch edges. Make second strap in same way.

2 Sew centre front seam of dungarees and press seam open. Position open end of straps against right side of dungarees at a slight angle. Baste each in place. Place facing right side to dungarees and sew from lower back edge at A across top and over to A on the other side.

3 Trim corners and turn facing right side out. Topstitch along edge just sewn. Clip seam allowance at A and sew dungarees together at centre back from A to match point beneath. (See Fig. b).

4 Press centre back and front seams open then sew inside leg seams. (See Fig. c). Turn dungarees right side out and fit on Kittens to determine length before hemming.

5 Finish dungarees by closing back waist edge with a hook and eye. Cross straps over at back and bring over shoulders to the front. Sew snaps on to straps and fix to dungarees. Sew fancy buttons to the top corners of the dungarees, covering the snaps.

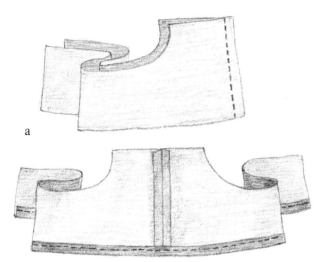

a

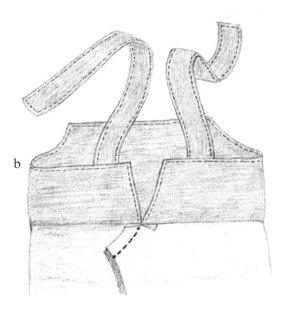

b

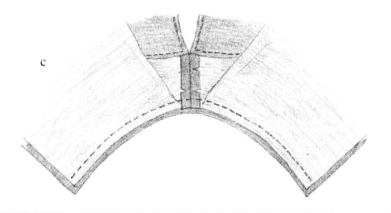

c

ABEARGAIL

*This bear cub makes clever use of the kitten pattern by
simply altering the shape of the ears and omitting the tail.
It completes a trio of dressed, clutch toys that make ideal
companions for young children because they are so very easy
to dress and undress with their one-piece outfits.*

MATERIALS NEEDED

50 cm × 68 cm (18 in × 27 in) fur
227 g (8 oz) stuffing
A pair of 16 mm amber safety eyes
Brown embroidery thread for nose
30.5 cm × 91 cm (12 in × 36 in)
  cotton print
2 snaps
2 small buttons

Height of Abeargail 29 cm (11 in)

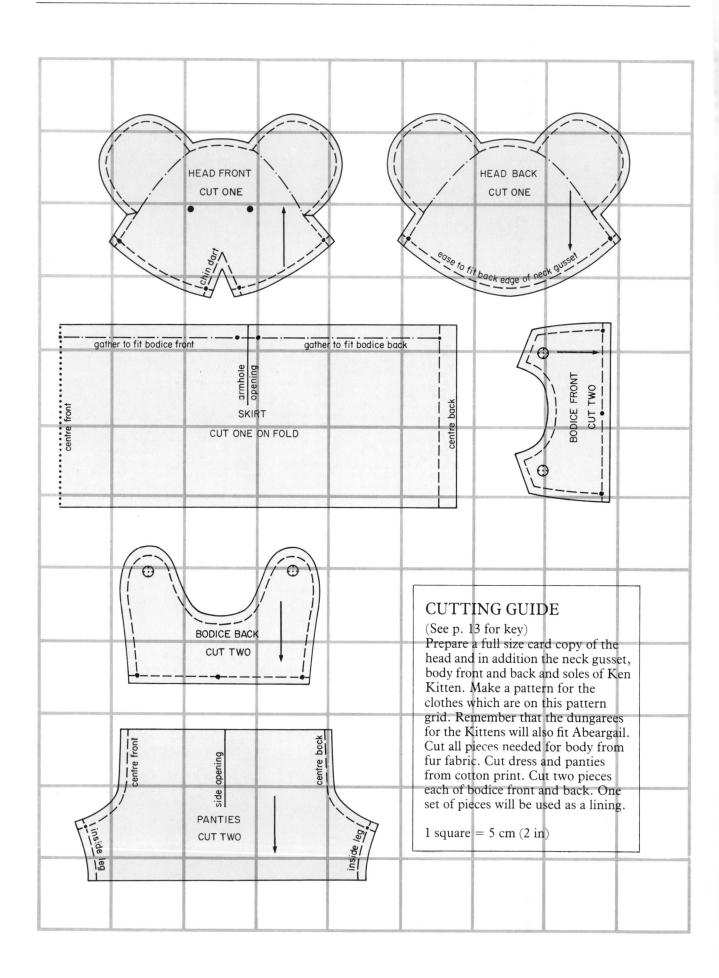

HEAD FRONT
CUT ONE

chin dart

HEAD BACK
CUT ONE

ease to fit back edge of neck gusset

gather to fit bodice front

armhole opening

gather to fit bodice back

centre front

centre back

SKIRT

CUT ONE ON FOLD

BODICE FRONT
CUT TWO

BODICE BACK

CUT TWO

centre front

side opening

centre back

PANTIES

CUT TWO

inside leg

inside leg

CUTTING GUIDE

(See p. 13 for key)
Prepare a full size card copy of the head and in addition the neck gusset, body front and back and soles of Ken Kitten. Make a pattern for the clothes which are on this pattern grid. Remember that the dungarees for the Kittens will also fit Abeargail. Cut all pieces needed for body from fur fabric. Cut dress and panties from cotton print. Cut two pieces each of bodice front and back. One set of pieces will be used as a lining.

1 square = 5 cm (2 in)

MAKING THE BODY

1 Follow the step-by-step instructions given for the Kittens (p. 138), omitting the tail. The nose is a block of brown satin stitches with a straight stitch mouth. Additional shaping to the head can be achieved by pulling the lower edge on the ears into the head and catching down with a stitch.

2 Neaten the edges of the side openings on both pieces of panties. Sew centre front and back seams. Clip seams and press open. (See Fig. a). Sew inside leg seams. Finish panties by making a narrow hem on each leg. Turn right side out and press. (See Fig. b).

3 Neaten the edges of the armholes on the skirt. Sew the centre back seam and neaten edges. Press seam open. Work a double row of gathering along the top front and back edges of the skirt. Place panties inside skirt with slits at the sides. Pull up gathering threads of skirt to fit front and back edges of panties then baste in position. (See Fig. c).

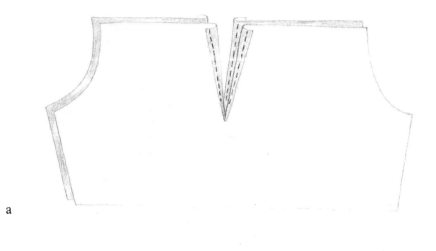

a

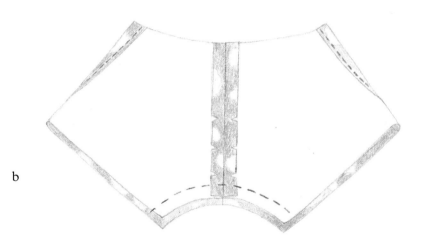

b

c

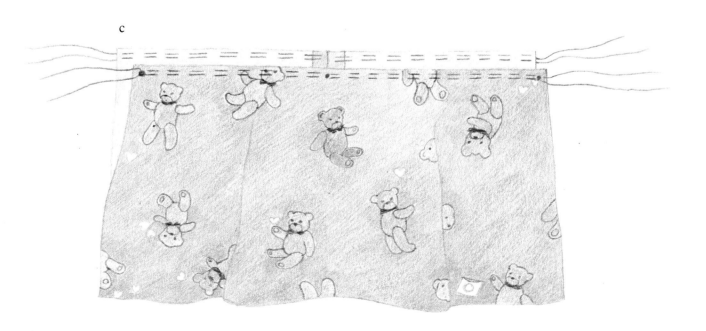

4 Take a set of bodice pieces and turn up lower edge at match points and press. Sew bodice front and lining together, clip and trim neck curve. Sew bodice back and lining together in same way as front. Turn both bodice pieces right side out and press.

5 Place right side of bodice back to back waist edge of skirt, with raw edges level. Match sides and centre, easing any fullness, baste then sew. Trim seam. Turn bodice up, tucking seam inside lining. Slipstitch lining in place along the seam line. Attach bodice front to skirt in the same way. (See Fig. d).

6 Sew snaps on bodice with back lapping over shoulders to lie on top at the front. Sew buttons on top of the snaps. (See Fig. e). Slip Abeargail feet first into her dress/pantie combination. Close snaps on shoulder then determine the required length. Remove dress and sew hem.

d

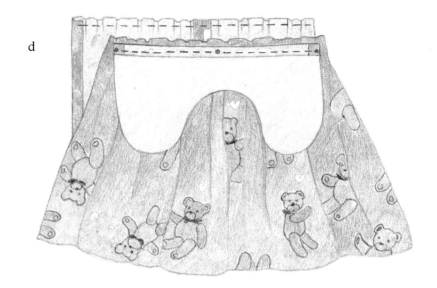

e

EDWARD AND EDWINA

*Teddy bears have appealed to both young and old alike
since their introduction slightly less than a hundred years
ago. Edward and Edwina might seem to be nostalgic
reminders of those early bears but they are thoroughly
modern in all respects. They do not have the long snout,
long arms, boot-button eyes or hump back of their ancestors.*

MATERIALS NEEDED TO MAKE BOTH BEARS

46 cm × 136 cm (18 in × 54 in) wide velour fur
340 g (12 oz) stuffing
2 pairs 12 mm dark brown safety eyes
23 cm (9 in) square of velvet for soles and paws
Brown DMC Perle Cotton for nose
4 large raincoat buttons, each with 4 holes

Height of each Bear 27 cm (10½ in)

MATERIALS NEEDED TO MAKE CLOTHES

46 cm × 92 cm (18 in × 36 in) wide blue and white
   strip cotton
46 cm × 115 cm (18 in × 45 in) wide white cotton
6 small buttons or snaps
1 m (1 yard) blue Russia braid
2 hooks and eyes
6 mm (¼ in) wide blue ribbon for ties
28 cm (11 in) narrow four cord elastic for legs
28 cm (11 in) of 6 mm (¼ in) wide elastic for waist

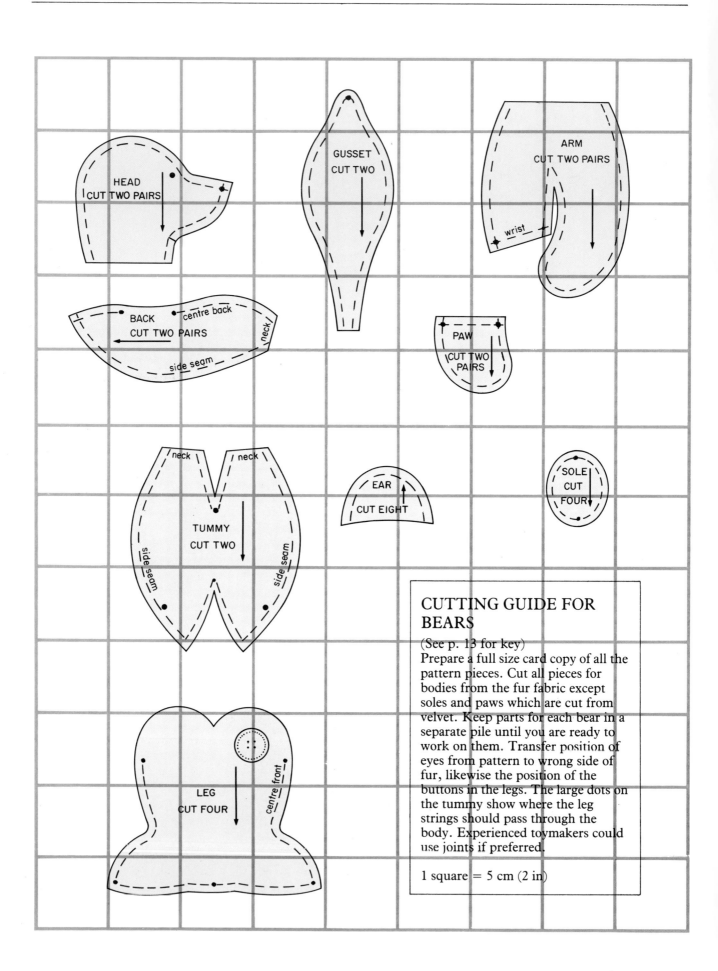

HEAD
CUT TWO PAIRS

GUSSET
CUT TWO

ARM
CUT TWO PAIRS

wrist

BACK
centre back
CUT TWO PAIRS
neck
side seam

PAW
CUT TWO
PAIRS

neck   neck

TUMMY
CUT TWO

side seam

side seam

EAR

CUT EIGHT

SOLE
CUT
FOUR

LEG
CUT FOUR

centre front

CUTTING GUIDE FOR BEARS

(See p. 13 for key)
Prepare a full size card copy of all the pattern pieces. Cut all pieces for bodies from the fur fabric except soles and paws which are cut from velvet. Keep parts for each bear in a separate pile until you are ready to work on them. Transfer position of eyes from pattern to wrong side of fur, likewise the position of the buttons in the legs. The large dots on the tummy show where the leg strings should pass through the body. Experienced toymakers could use joints if preferred.

1 square = 5 cm (2 in)

MAKING THE BODY

1 Sew paws to wrist edges of arms with raw edges level. Turn paws up and finger press seams open. (See Fig. a). Fold arm in half lengthways and baste curved edge before sewing from shoulder down around paw. Make remaining arms in same way checking that you have pairs. Turn arms right side out and stuff nearly to the top. Too much stuffing will cause arms to be raised when attached to the body.

2 Sew buttons in position on inside of hips with strong thread. Feed a small safety pin through the stitches on the outside. This will help you locate the buttons when attaching the legs to the body. Fold leg in half lengthways and sew between match points on centre front. Complete all legs in the same way checking that you have made two pairs. (See Fig. b).

3 Pin soles in place, baste then sew by hand, using a small back stitch. Turn legs right side out after clipping seam allowance at the ankles. Stuff firmly and close openings at top. Fold each tummy piece in half and sew the darts on the centre front from match points to edges. (See Fig. c). Sew back pieces together down centre back leaving central stretch between match points open. Sew fronts to backs, leaving neck edge open.

a

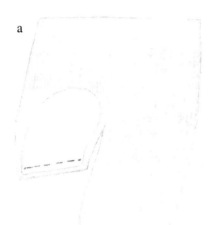

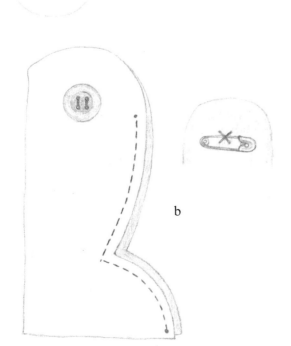

b

c

4 Turn completed body right side out and stuff firmly. Lay body on table with tummy facing you and position a leg on each side ready for assembly. Using strong double thread, string bear together by passing needle under stitches of leg on one side, through body, under stitches of leg of other side and back through body to the start. Leave threads hanging as shown. Now repeat the stringing but this time start on the opposite side. Tie pairs of threads together on each side in turn, in reef knots, pulling up tightly as you do it. This should pull the legs in close to the body. Take threads back into body and tie them all together again through the opening in the back. Close back opening with ladder stitch.

5 Press top edges of an arm together and sew securely to the neck edge of the body. Sew on other arm in same way and check that paws face forward. (See Fig. d). Sew head pieces together in pairs from nose down to neck edge. Clip seam allowance under chin.

6 Pin and baste gusset between sides of head, then, when satisfied that both sides are evenly spaced, sew in place. (See Fig. e). Turn head right side out, insert safety eyes and stuff firmly. Turn under neck edge and slightly gather. Place head on top of body, hold in place with long darning needles and ladderstitch in place.

7 Sew ears together in pairs. This is neater if done by hand after first basting the edges. Turn right side out and whip bottom edges together. Clean seams now. Position ear on head and hold in place with long, glass headed pins. Spread the base and arrange in a slight curve. Ladderstitch across back of ear first then the front, this will pull the ear forward. Sew remaining ears in place. By now your bears will have slight differences even though you have made them both the same way. Take this opportunity to make one look more like Edward and the other like the little girl, Edwina.

8 Work a block of satin stitches horizontally across gusset to embroider the nose. Bring thread out at A and insert needle at B and out at C, looping thread over point of needle. Pull thread through at C to draw up mouth stitches, pass needle in at base of nose and backstitch away to finish off. Complete nose and mouth showing small stitch that locks mouth stitch in place at bottom of nose.

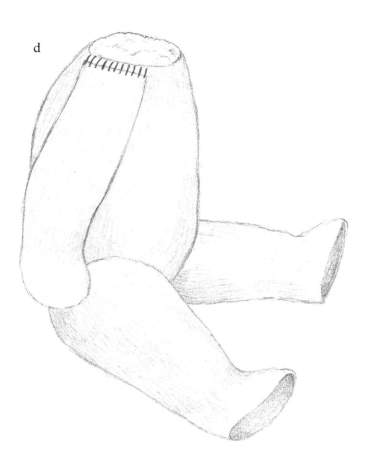

d

e

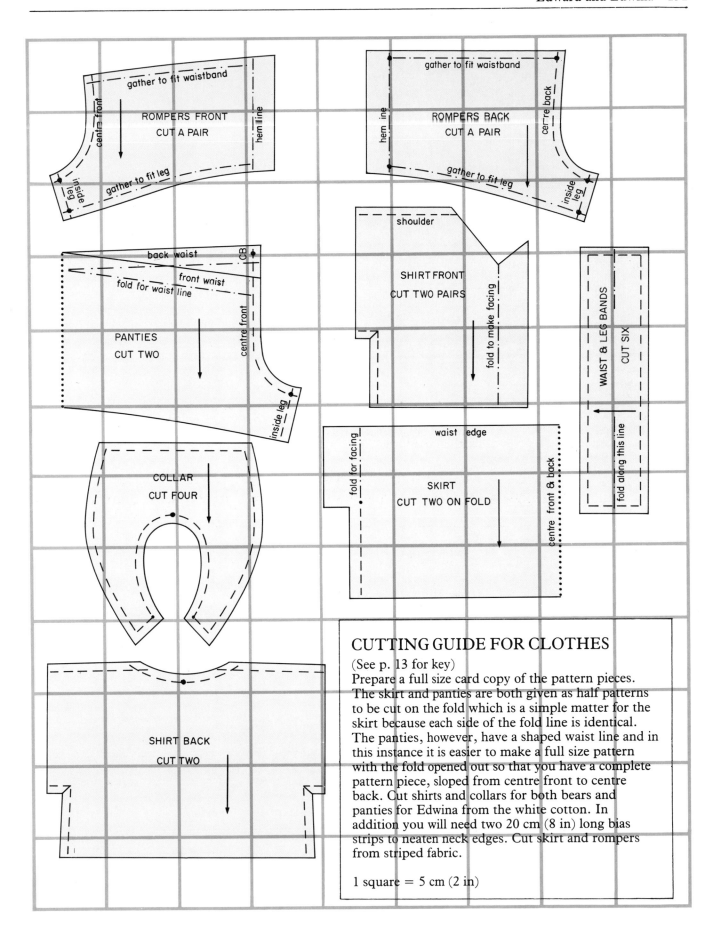

ROMPERS FRONT
CUT A PAIR

gather to fit waistband

centre front

hem line

inside leg

gather to fit leg

ROMPERS BACK
CUT A PAIR

gather to fit waistband

hem line

centre back

inside leg

gather to fit leg

back waist

front waist

fold for waist line

CB

PANTIES
CUT TWO

centre front

inside leg

shoulder

SHIRT FRONT
CUT TWO PAIRS

fold to make facing

WAIST & LEG BANDS
CUT SIX

fold along this line

fold for facing

waist edge

SKIRT
CUT TWO ON FOLD

centre front & back

COLLAR
CUT FOUR

SHIRT BACK
CUT TWO

CUTTING GUIDE FOR CLOTHES

(See p. 13 for key)

Prepare a full size card copy of the pattern pieces. The skirt and panties are both given as half patterns to be cut on the fold which is a simple matter for the skirt because each side of the fold line is identical. The panties, however, have a shaped waist line and in this instance it is easier to make a full size pattern with the fold opened out so that you have a complete pattern piece, sloped from centre front to centre back. Cut shirts and collars for both bears and panties for Edwina from the white cotton. In addition you will need two 20 cm (8 in) long bias strips to neaten neck edges. Cut skirt and rompers from striped fabric.

1 square = 5 cm (2 in)

MAKING THE CLOTHES

1 Start making the rompers by sewing fronts together at the centre front. Neaten each side with a narrow double hem. Press seam and clip curve. (See Fig. a).

2 Gather front waist edge to fit between side seams of Edward's body. Sew waistband to waist edge, raw edges level. Leave a small overlap at each end. Press seam downwards and fold waistband in half with right sides together. Sew both short ends and overlaps. Clip corners off then turn waistband right side out. Fold seam upwards into band and slipstitch opening closed.

3 Make back of rompers in the same way as the front but trim off the overlap from the waistband. Sew front and back together along the inside leg seams. Run a gathering thread from side to side along each leg edge. Pull up to fit the legs of the bear, adjusting the gathers to spread the fullness evenly. Work buttonholes on front waistband and sew buttons on back. Alternatively, sew on snaps. (See Fig. b).

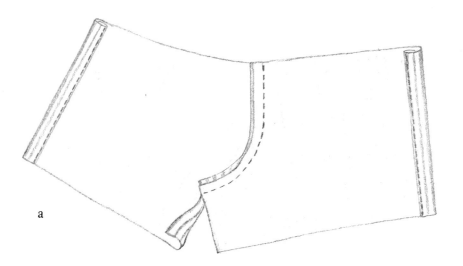

a

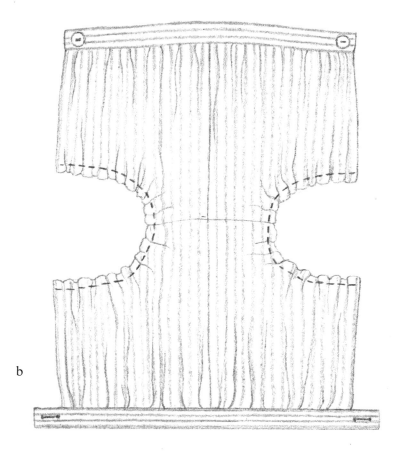

b

4 Sew leg bands on in the same way as the waist bands. Leave a small overlap at the front edge and none at the back. Complete rompers by working buttonholes on front overlaps and sew buttons on back ends. (See Fig. c).

5 Make panties for Edwina by joining pieces together at centre front and back. Press seams open and clip curves. Make a casing for the elastic at the waist by turning under the edge and then folding down again along the waistline. Sew, leaving a small opening at the centre back. (See Fig. d).

6 Topstitch folded edge of waist then thread a length of elastic through the casing. Pull up to fit bear and sew ends together securely. Slipstitch opening closed.

7 Make a narrower casing on both leg edges. Thread elastic through each casing. Sew elastic securely in place in front inside leg edges then pull up each piece in turn to fit legs and anchor other end in place securely in same way. Finish panties by folding to bring centre front and back together and sewing the inside leg seams. Trim and turn the panties right side out.

8 Neaten both front edges of shirt then fold over facings and baste to neck edge. Sew fronts to back at shoulder and press seams open. Make narrow hems on each sleeve. Join two collar sections together around outer edge leaving inside neck edge open. Clip seams, trim corners, turn right side out and press.

9 Decorate collar with Russia braid. Tuck ends under collar front edges and sew braid in place through centre channel. Lay collar on right side of shirt with raw neck edges level. Sew from front around neck to front on other side. (See Fig. e).

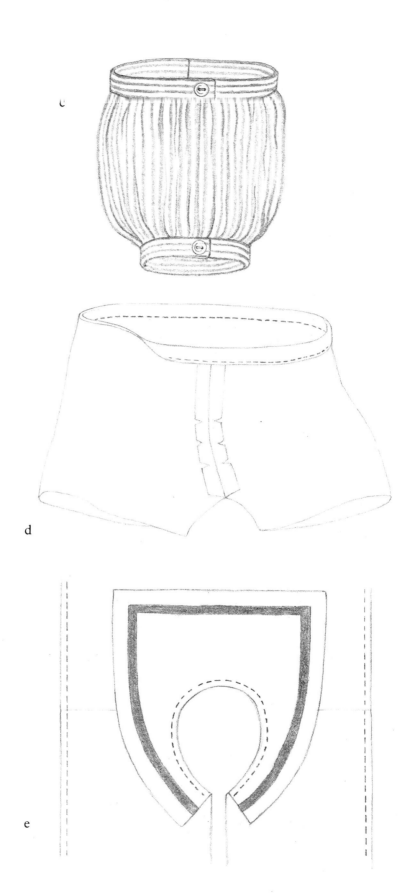

10 Take a length of bias and sew around neck edge along seam line just made. Fold each end of bias to top to neaten. Trim neck edge carefully and clip at regular intervals to release tension. Neaten raw edge of bias, press seam and bias strip towards shirt and pull collar away from shirt. Now stitch carefully along neck edge of shirt through all thickness of shirt, collar seam and facing.

11 Catch front ends of bias facing down to shirt front facing. Fold shirt and sew under arm and side seams on each side, clip corners and press seams. Open out front facings at lower edge of shirt and turn up hem then fold facing back on top of hem and sew in place either by machine or hand. (See Fig. f).

12 Sew a hook and eye on either side of front, just under the collar. Now tie a blue bow and sew in place on one side at front neck edge to hide hook and eye. Make a second shirt in the same way.

13 Neaten all edges of skirt facings. Make a total of six pleats on front of skirt with two on each side of a central box pleat. Make pleats on back skirt in same way. Baste in place. Alternatively, gather waist edges to fit Edwina's body. Sew side seams from match points down to bottom edge.

14 Press side seams open together with facings formed at the top of the seams. Sew waistbands to front and back of skirt in the same way as described for the rompers. Sew snaps on either side of waistband or finish with buttons and buttonholes as you wish. Fit skirt on Edwina and determine the required length. Remove skirt, hem, press and finally dress back on bear.

f

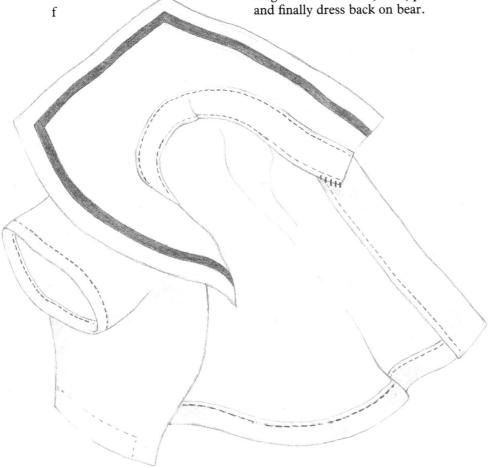

MELISSA MOUSE

Melissa, costumed as she is, captures all the charm of an old world, country-style mouse. To complete her wardrobe there are lace trimmed lawn drawers and petticoat. The softness of the character is further enhanced by a set of very fine whiskers, a tail that peeps out from between the clothes and a big pink satin bow to tie under her chin.

MATERIALS NEEDED

50 cm × 136 cm (18 in × 54 in) wide fur fabric
30.5 cm (12 in) square of flesh coloured felt
A pair of 18 mm brown safety eyes
340 g (12 oz) stuffing
Nylon thread for whiskers

Height of Mouse 43 cm (17 in)

MATERIALS NEEDED FOR CLOTHES

60 cm × 115 cm (24 in × 45 in) wide
 white lawn
92 cm × 92 cm (36 in × 36 in) wide
 cotton print
5 m (5 yards) cotton lace
1 m (1 yard) of 2.5 cm (1 in) wide
 pink satin ribbon
3 small buttons
5 snaps
2 m (2 yards) of 6 mm (¼ in) wide
 elastic

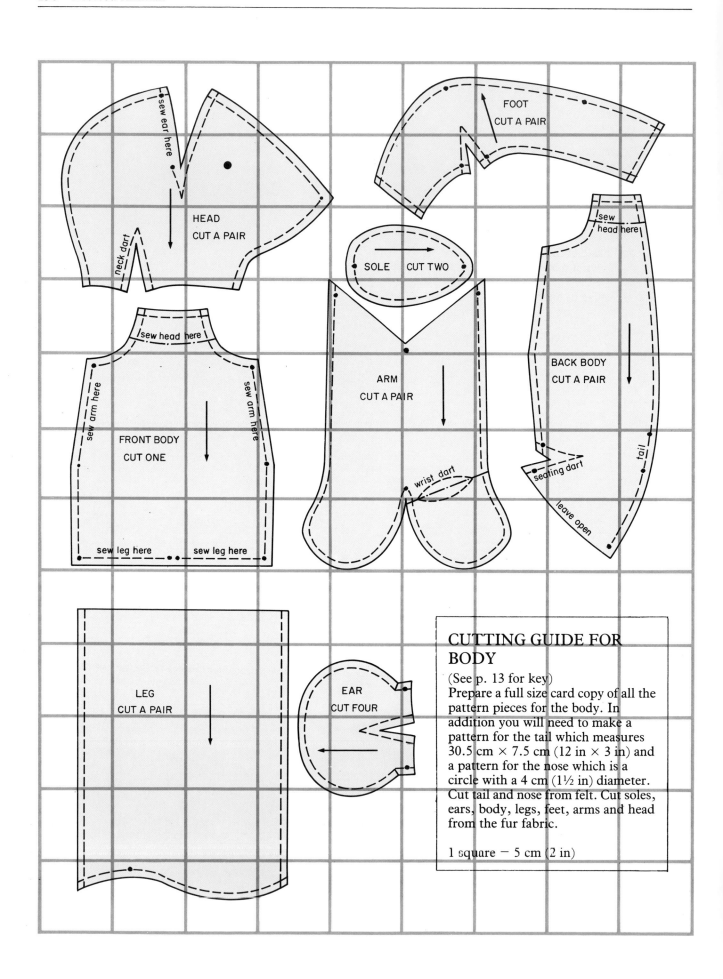

FOOT
CUT A PAIR

sew ear here

HEAD
CUT A PAIR

neck dart

sew head here

SOLE   CUT TWO

BACK BODY
CUT A PAIR

sew head here

sew arm here

sew arm here

FRONT BODY
CUT ONE

ARM
CUT A PAIR

wrist dart

seating dart

tail

leave open

sew leg here   sew leg here

LEG
CUT A PAIR

EAR
CUT FOUR

CUTTING GUIDE FOR BODY

(See p. 13 for key)
Prepare a full size card copy of all the pattern pieces for the body. In addition you will need to make a pattern for the tail which measures 30.5 cm × 7.5 cm (12 in × 3 in) and a pattern for the nose which is a circle with a 4 cm (1½ in) diameter. Cut tail and nose from felt. Cut soles, ears, body, legs, feet, arms and head from the fur fabric.

1 square − 5 cm (2 in)

MAKING THE BODY

1 Fold paw upwards along guideline marked on pattern and sew curved wrist dart. Turn paw down and fold arm in half lengthways. Baste edges together before sewing from shoulder down around paw.

2 Turn arm right side out and stuff to within 3 cm (1¼ in) of the top. Hold stuffing in place with a glass-headed pin. Make second arm in same way and baste both arms to front body with wrist darts against front. (See Fig. a).

3 Fold lower edge of back upwards to sew the seating dart. Repeat on other side. Sew backs to front down each side from neck edge to seating darts. This encloses the arms in a swing hinge. (See Fig. b).

4 Make tail by folding felt strip in half lengthways, twice. Sew the outline from one end of the length to taper at the other. Trim away excess felt with sharp scissors. Refold body to sew centre back seam with tail in position between match points. Press neck edges together and sew across from side to side.

5 Make darts on top of each foot piece. Finger press foot dart open and sew foot to base of leg with raw edges level. Refold leg and foot lengthways. Sew inside leg seam. (See Fig. c). Position sole, baste, then sew in place by hand with a small back stitch. Turn leg right side out, clean seams and stuff firmly nearly to the top. Hold stuffing in place as directed for the arms. Make second leg in same way checking that you have a pair.

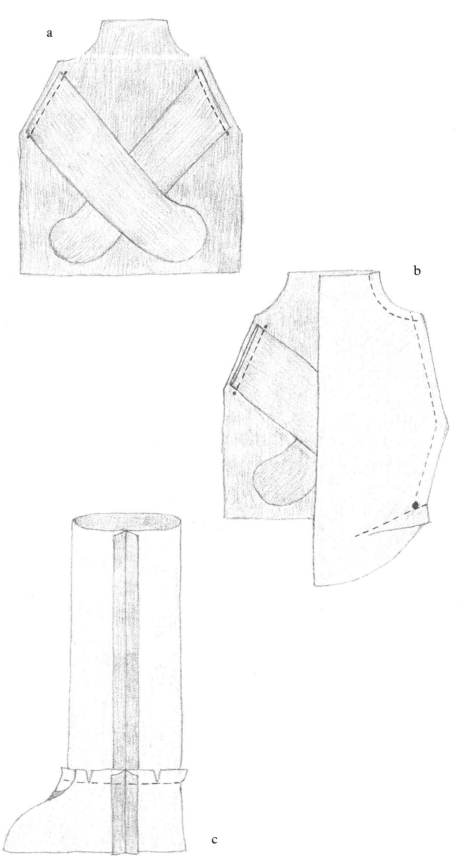

6 Turn body right side out. Remove pins from arms. Baste legs in position against lower front edge. Check that toes face forwards and that leg seams lie together on the inside. When satisfied with the appearance and length of legs, sew them securely to the body. Stuff body through lower back opening then ladderstitch from to back. Remove pins from top of legs. (See Fig. d).

7 Make darts in all ear pieces. Finger press darts open then sew ears together in pairs. Clip corners and turn right side out. Baste an ear to the back edge of ear dart on both head pieces. Sew darts, enclosing base of ears. Sew neck darts on each head piece and press open.

8 Sew head together from neck edge at front to neck edge at back taking care not to trap ears in seam. Turn head right side out and insert safety eyes. Stuff head firmly. Turn under neck edge and partly draw up with a strong gathering thread. Work your fingers into the stuffing and make a cavity just large enough to fit the neck stump on the body. Pull head down on to body and ladderstitch in place, securely. (See Fig. e).

9 Run a gathering thread round the edge of the felt nose. Start to pull up on the gathering thread to make a ball, enclose enough stuffing to mould a firm shape. Finish off gathering and ladderstitch nose in place on snout. Finally, work a few whiskers on each side. Trim to required shape.

d

e

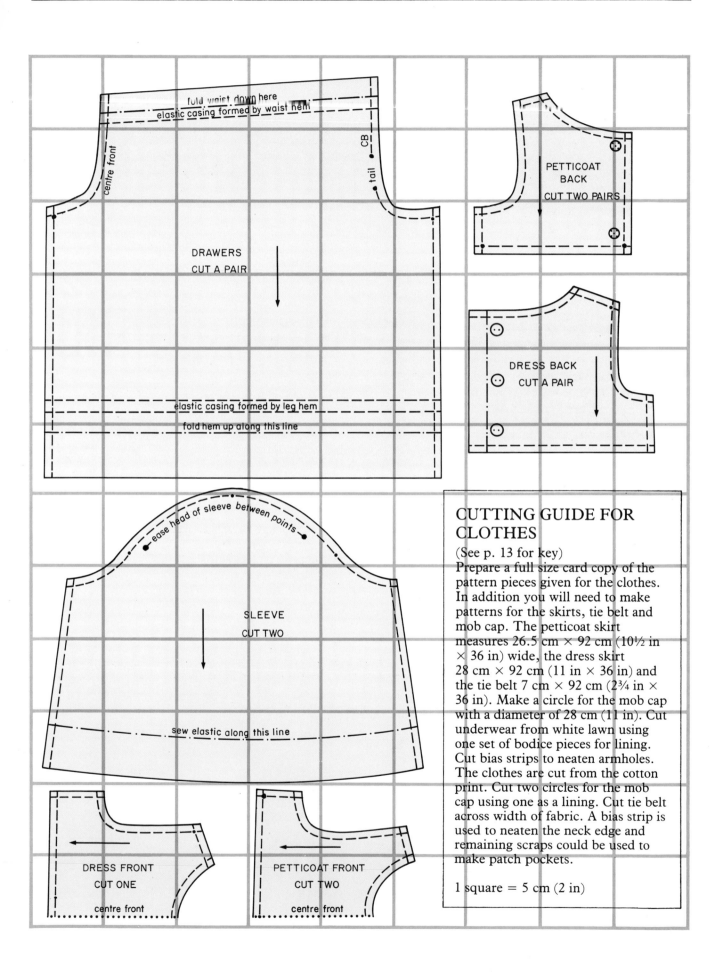

fold waist down here
elastic casing formed by waist hem

centre front

CB

tail

DRAWERS
CUT A PAIR

elastic casing formed by leg hem
fold hem up along this line

PETTICOAT
BACK
CUT TWO PAIRS

DRESS BACK
CUT A PAIR

ease head of sleeve between points

SLEEVE
CUT TWO

sew elastic along this line

DRESS FRONT
CUT ONE
centre front

PETTICOAT FRONT
CUT TWO
centre front

CUTTING GUIDE FOR CLOTHES
(See p. 13 for key)
Prepare a full size card copy of the pattern pieces given for the clothes. In addition you will need to make patterns for the skirts, tie belt and mob cap. The petticoat skirt measures 26.5 cm × 92 cm (10½ in × 36 in) wide, the dress skirt 28 cm × 92 cm (11 in × 36 in) and the tie belt 7 cm × 92 cm (2¾ in × 36 in). Make a circle for the mob cap with a diameter of 28 cm (11 in). Cut underwear from white lawn using one set of bodice pieces for lining. Cut bias strips to neaten armholes. The clothes are cut from the cotton print. Cut two circles for the mob cap using one as a lining. Cut tie belt across width of fabric. A bias strip is used to neaten the neck edge and remaining scraps could be used to make patch pockets.

1 square = 5 cm (2 in)

MAKING THE CLOTHES

1 Sew centre back seam of drawers leaving an opening between match points. Clip seam and press open. Topstitch edge of tail opening on right side. Refold drawers and sew centre front seam. Clip and press seam open. (See Fig. a).

2 Bring inside edges of legs together and sew each side of the crotch in turn. Press under 3 mm (⅛ in) on waist edge. Press edge to inside along fold line to form a casing. Stitch close to both edges of casing, leaving an opening at centre back on inner seam line to insert elastic. Thread elastic through casing and adjust to fit. Cut off excess. Overlap ends of elastic and sew together securely. Slipstitch opening closed.

3 Press a narrow fold along leg edge then turn up along fold line to make a deep hem. Sew, leaving an opening at the inside leg seam. The casing is made within the hem by sewing another line 12 mm (½ in) beneath. Sew lace to lower edge of leg. Thread elastic through casing, pull up to required length, trim surplus and sew ends together securely. Close opening. Complete other leg in same way. Press drawers and fit on Melissa, threading tail through opening.

4 To make the petticoat, sew backs to front on shoulders and press both seams open. Make bodice lining in same way and place lining and bodice right sides together. Sew from waist up back, round neck and down back to waist on other side. Trim seam, clip curve, turn right side out and press neck edge carefully. (See Fig. b). Sew bodice side seams in turn, then lining side seams. Press all four seams open.

5 Hem both short sides and lower edge of petticoat skirt. Decorate lower edge with lace. Gather waist edge of skirt and pull up to fit bodice. With raw edges level and right sides together match centre front of skirt to centre front of bodice front and back edges of skirt to sides of bodice. Keep lining folded out of way at this stage. Adjust gathers, spreading fullness evenly.

Sew skirt to bodice. Turn seam up inside bodice and slipstitch lining to waist seam line.

6 Finish petticoat by neatening armhole edges with bias binding. Sew snaps to close back opening at neck and waist. The bottom of the petticoat is left open for easy dressing by little hands.

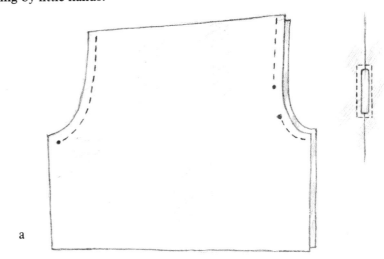

a

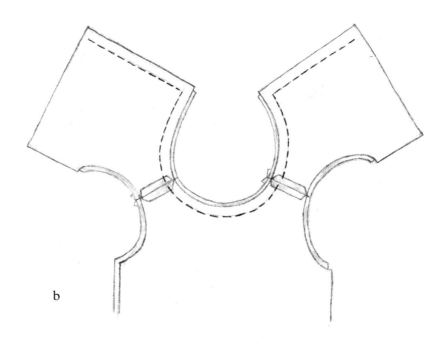

b

7 Sew bodice front and backs of dress together at shoulders, press seams open. Prepare each sleeve by gathering the head between side match points. Pull up on gathering threads until sleeve fits armhole opening. Adjust gathers, spreading the fullness evenly. With right sides togeter and raw edges level, pin and baste a sleeve in place matching shoulder seam to centre of sleeve head. Sew. (See Fig. c). Attach second sleeve to bodice in same way. Trim seams and clip to release tension on curves.

8 Neaten each wrist edge of sleeve with a narrow hem and decorate with a row of lace. Check length of dressing on Melissa and making any necessary adjustments.

9 Stretch a length of elastic across the placement line and sew in place. Fold sleeve, right side inside, to bring underarm edges together. Sew a continuous underarm and side bodice seam. Clip corner. Sew underarm seam on other side of bodice in same way.

10 Work two rows of gathering at waist edge of skirt. Pull up to fit waist edge of bodice. Pin at centre fronts and sides spreading gathers evenly. Baste then sew. Hem both back edges of dress from neck to lower skirt edge. Put dress on mouse and mark length. Hem lower edge and decorate with lace. Finish neck edge by neatening with a bias strip. (See Fig. d).

11 Sew buttons to back opening and work buttonholes or sew snaps under buttons as an alternative. Fold tie belt in half lengthwise and sew both short ends and most of the length. Leave a 5 cm (2 in) opening. Trim corners and turn right side out. Close opening and press. Topstitch all round edge of belt. Centre belt on front of bodice and topstitch it in place to bodice beneath. Tie in a bow at the back.

12 With raw edges level, sew lace round edge of one mob cap section. Place lining section right side to lace trimmed section. Sew together round edge leaving an opening. Turn right side out, close opening and press.

13 Fold mob cap in half and half again to locate the centre. Mark with crossed pins. Open cap out flat and lay on table, lining uppermost. Tack the outline of an 18 cm (7¼ in) diameter circle in the centre of the cap. Stretch elastic along this line and sew in place. Check that cap is a comfortable fit then sew a length of satin ribbon on each side on the elastic line. Tie cap under chin. (See Fig. e).

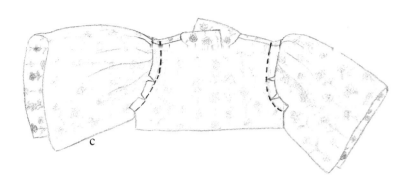

c

d

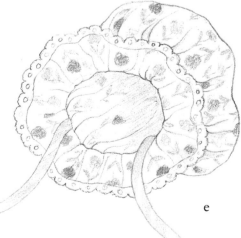

e

HARRIET HARE

Harriet, like Melissa, is another country-style character and, with her long elegant ears tipped with black, must be a hare. She is wearing a washing bonnet, so called because it opens out flat for easy laundering. They were very popular with little girls at the turn of the last century.

MATERIALS NEEDED

50 cm × 137 cm (18 in × 54 in) wide beige fur
30.5 cm (12 in) square of white fur
A small piece of black fur
A pair of 16.5 mm amber safety eyes
340 g (12 oz) stuffing
Embroidery thread for nose
92 cm × 92 cm (36 in × 36 in) wide cotton print
60 cm × 114 cm (24 in × 45 in) wide white lawn
30.5 cm × 92 cm (12 in × 36 in) wide eyelet embroidery
152 cm (5 ft) cotton lace for underwear
137 cm (1½ yards) of 6 mm (¼ in) wide ribbon for bonnet
75 cm (30 in) of 4 cm (1½ in) wide cotton lace for bonnet
51 cm (20 in) lace for apron
3 small buttons
5 snaps

Height of Hare 56 cm (22 in)

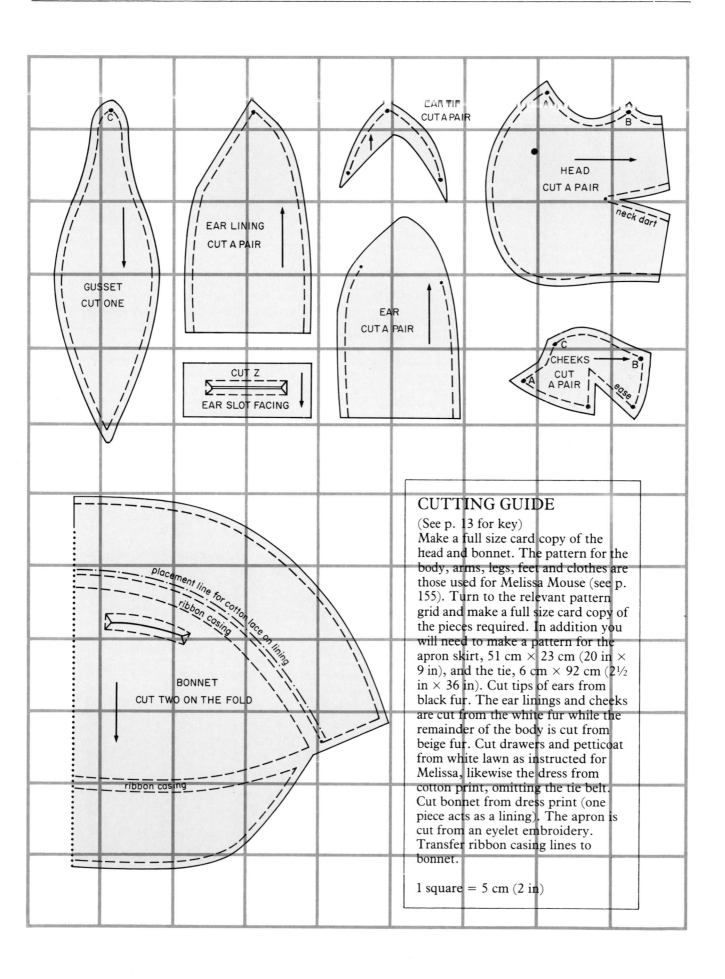

CUTTING GUIDE

(See p. 13 for key)

Make a full size card copy of the head and bonnet. The pattern for the body, arms, legs, feet and clothes are those used for Melissa Mouse (see p. 155). Turn to the relevant pattern grid and make a full size card copy of the pieces required. In addition you will need to make a pattern for the apron skirt, 51 cm × 23 cm (20 in × 9 in), and the tie, 6 cm × 92 cm (2½ in × 36 in). Cut tips of ears from black fur. The ear linings and cheeks are cut from the white fur while the remainder of the body is cut from beige fur. Cut drawers and petticoat from white lawn as instructed for Melissa, likewise the dress from cotton print, omitting the tie belt. Cut bonnet from dress print (one piece acts as a lining). The apron is cut from an eyelet embroidery. Transfer ribbon casing lines to bonnet.

1 square = 5 cm (2 in)

MAKING THE BODY

1 Start by making the darts on the cheeks. Run a gathering thread along the long side of the dart and pull up to fit. Close dart by working a small back stitch. Check that the cheeks made are a pair. Sew darts at neck edge at each head section. Now sew cheeks to head matching As and Bs and easing the curve to fit.

2 Sew heads together from nose at C through B to neck edge. (See Fig. a). Pin gusset between head pieces starting at C and work back to neck edge, on each side in turn. Be careful not to stretch the curves. Baste then sew.

3 Turn head right side out and insert safety eyes. Stuff head, carefully shaping the cheeks. Turn under neck edge and slightly gather to draw up neck. Finish Harriet by making a body as outlined for Melissa, remembering that she does not need the long tail. Sew head securely to body.

4 Sew black tip to ear by hand. Start at the centre top and oversew down one side, back up to start, down other side and finally back to top. This results in a very narrow seam. Make other ear in same way. Sew ears to linings, leaving base open. Turn right side out and fold lengthwise. Sew bottom edges together. Check that you have made a pair.

5 Position ears on head and hold in place with glass-headed pins. Ladderstitch in place across front first and then the back. (See Fig. b). Embroider a satin stitch nose and straight stitch mouth.

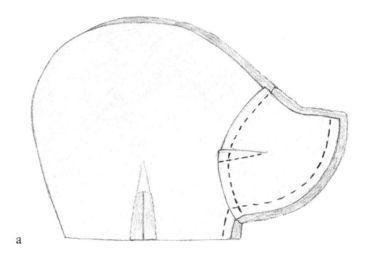

a

b

MAKING THE CLOTHES

6 Follow the instructions given for Melissa Mouse to make the underwear (p. 155), omitting the opening for the tail. The dress is decorated with two rows of ric-rac round the bottom of the skirt and a single row round each wrist edge.

7 Sew bonnet and lining together round edge, leaving open between match points on each side. Clip curve, trim corners and turn right side out. Turn in raw edges of the openings and press. Topstitch ribbon casing lines on bonnet through both layers. Slipstitch any opening left at the sides that is not needed for the casings.

8 Press and sew under a narrow turning round all sides of both ear slot facings. Position the facings right sides to outside of bonnet. Sew round each slot, squaring off the corners. Clip corners. Push facings through respective slots to lining side of bonnet. Hem or topstitch in place. (See Fig. c).

9 Press under a narrow turning on each end of bonnet lace. Neaten long edge if necessary and gather to fit bonnet brim. Position on placement line on lining, just in front of ribbon casing. Spread gathers evenly and sew in place. Sew ends to edges of brim. Thread a metre length of ribbon through each casing. Pull up on ribbons to shape bonnet, place on head and tie ribbons together under chin in a bow. (See Fig. d).

10 Make a narrow hem on all sides of the apron. Decorate the lower edge with lace. Gather apron to fit waist by working a double row of gathering 2.5 cm (1 in) beneath waist edge. Fold apron tie in half widthwise and sew short ends and most of the length, leaving a small opening. Trim corners and turn right side out. Close opening and press. Position tie over apron and sew in place. Dress apron on Harriet and tie in a bow at the back. (See Fig. e).

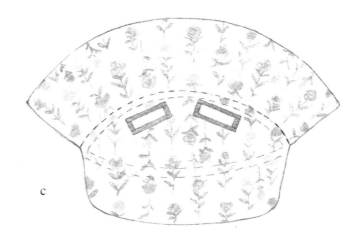

c

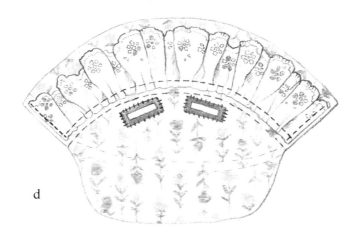

d

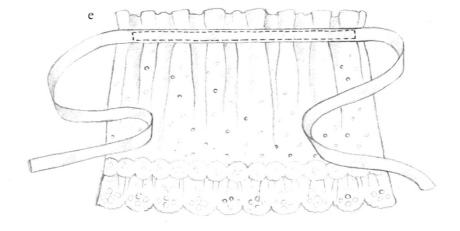

e

BROCK THE BADGER

Brock completes the trio of country-style characters that share the same basic body pattern although in this instance he is made from black and white flecked tweed rather than fur. Brock is dressed in woodland green velvet trousers, modern checked smock and a small felt beret. Remember that the clothes are interchangeable for these animals.

MATERIALS NEEDED FOR THE BODY

30.5 cm × 115 cm (12 in × 45 in) wide tweed
30.5 cm (12 in) square of unpolished white fur
30.5 cm (12 in) square of wild animal badger fur
30.5 cm (12 in) square of black fur
340 g (12 oz) stuffing
A pair of 16 mm brown safety eyes
A small piece of black satin for nose
A scrap of black felt for ears

Height of Badger 48 cm (19 in)

MATERIALS NEEDED FOR THE CLOTHES

30.5 cm × 115 cm (12 in × 45 in) wide green velvet
46 cm × 92 cm (18 in × 36 in) wide check cotton
30.5 cm (12 in) square of green felt
4 trouser and 3 shirt buttons
5 snaps and a hook and eye
Bias binding to neaten trousers

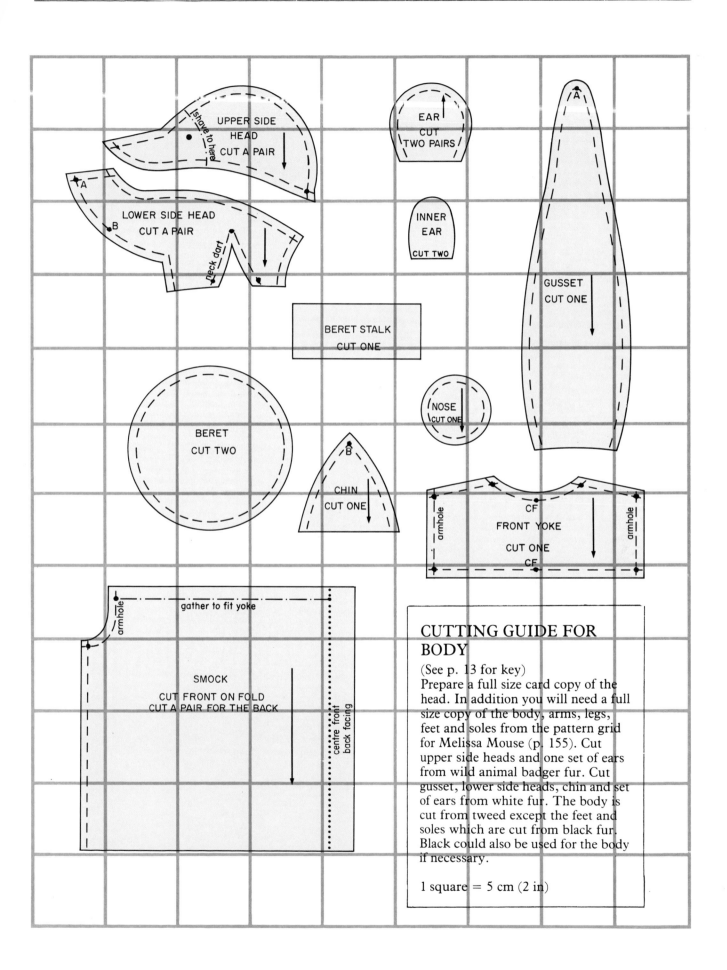

UPPER SIDE
HEAD
CUT A PAIR

shave to here

LOWER SIDE HEAD
CUT A PAIR

A

B

neck dart

EAR
CUT
TWO PAIRS

INNER
EAR
CUT TWO

A

GUSSET
CUT ONE

BERET STALK
CUT ONE

BERET
CUT TWO

NOSE
CUT ONE

B

CHIN
CUT ONE

armhole

CF

FRONT YOKE

CUT ONE

CF

armhole

armhole

gather to fit yoke

SMOCK

CUT FRONT ON FOLD
CUT A PAIR FOR THE BACK

centre front

back facing

CUTTING GUIDE FOR BODY

(See p. 13 for key)
Prepare a full size card copy of the head. In addition you will need a full size copy of the body, arms, legs, feet and soles from the pattern grid for Melissa Mouse (p. 155). Cut upper side heads and one set of ears from wild animal badger fur. Cut gusset, lower side heads, chin and set of ears from white fur. The body is cut from tweed except the feet and soles which are cut from black fur. Black could also be used for the body if necessary.

1 square = 5 cm (2 in)

MAKING THE BODY

1 Make a body for Brock by following the instructions given for Melissa (p. 155). Shave the fur carefully from the snout of the upper side heads. As the long pile is removed, the fur will become darker. Don't over-trim at this stage, because you can always shave more when the head is made up.

2 Pin and baste upper side heads to lower side heads, taking care not to stretch the curves. Sew. Make darts on neck edge. Sew head sections right sides together from A to B. Fit chin between head sections and baste from B to neck edge on each side in turn before sewing. Clip corners. (See Fig. a).

3 Pin and baste gusset to top of head. Sew. Turn head right side out and insert safety eyes. Stuff. Turn under neck edge and gather slightly to draw neck opening inwards. Pull head down on to neck stump and ladderstitch to body.

4 Topstitch a black felt inner ear piece to each white front ear. Shave the pile from the ear backs then baste and sew front and back ears together. Turn ears right side out, clean seams and baste open edges together by whipping. Position ears on upper side heads, gently teasing long pile apart to snuggle base of ears close to head. Ladderstitch in place. (See Fig. b).

5 Gather edge of nose circle and pull up tightly, fasten off. Press nose disc flat. Place on end of snout and pin at quarters. Gradually work excess towards lower half until you can make a small pleat on each side to form the nostrils. When satisfied with the appearance, hem in place, inserting a little stuffing to give it a firm shape.

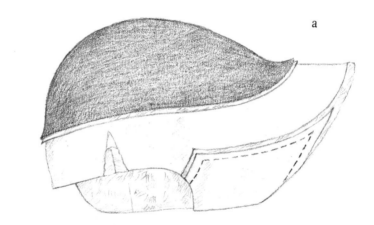

a

b

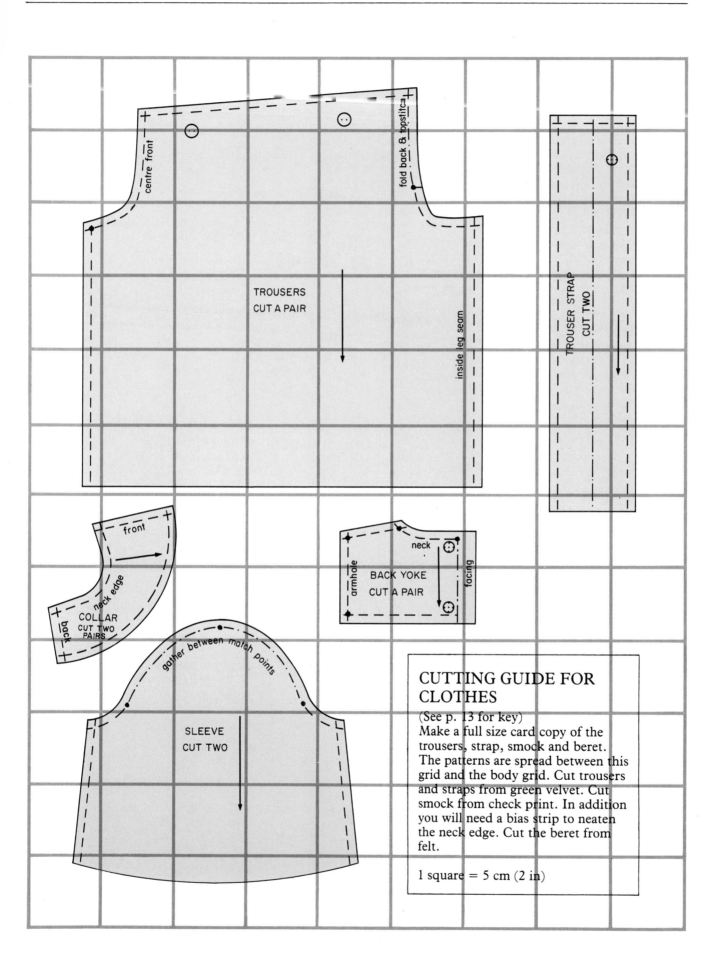

centre front

fold back & topstitch

TROUSERS
CUT A PAIR

inside leg seam

TROUSER STRAP
CUT TWO

front

neck edge

COLLAR
CUT TWO
PAIRS

back

neck

armhole

BACK YOKE
CUT A PAIR

facing

gather between match points

SLEEVE
CUT TWO

CUTTING GUIDE FOR CLOTHES

(See p. 13 for key)
Make a full size card copy of the trousers, strap, smock and beret. The patterns are spread between this grid and the body grid. Cut trousers and straps from green velvet. Cut smock from check print. In addition you will need a bias strip to neaten the neck edge. Cut the beret from felt.

1 square = 5 cm (2 in)

MAKING THE CLOTHES

1 Sew centre front seams of trousers and lower centre back between the match points. Clip curves. Neaten remainder of centre back by pressing seam allowance open and topstitching each side. (See Fig. a).

2 Refold trousers to sew inside leg seams, taking care to match centre front and back seams. Neaten leg edges by hemming with a cotton bias strip. Neaten waist edge in same way.

3 Fold each strap in half lengthwise and sew one short end and long side. Turn right side out, press and topstitch edges. Sew raw ends of straps to front of trousers and sew buttons in place.

4 Dress trousers on badger, cross straps over at back to determine the fit. Sew snaps in place to close straps at back and then sew buttons on trousers to match those in front. Close back opening at waist with hook and eye. (See Fig. b).

5 Gather front and backs of smock to fit front and back yoke sections respectively. Sew backs to front on shoulder seams, press open. (See Fig. c). Gather head of sleeves between match points. Pull up to fit armhole opening and sew in place.

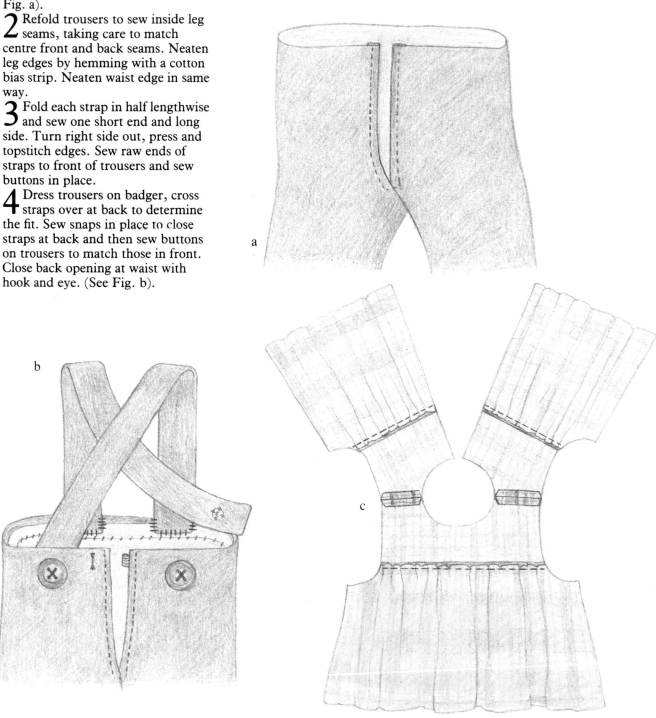

6 Make a narrow double hem on each wrist edge of sleeve. Fold smock to sew a continuous underarm and side seam to lower smock edge. Repeat on other side. Clip corners. Make a narrow double hem down back edges of smock, from neck to bottom. Hem bottom of smock.

7 Sew collars together. Trim corners, clip curve and turn right side out. Press. Place collars against neck edge with deeper part of collars meeting at centre front. Sew. Sew a bias strip against this neck edge, remembering to fold over ends. Neaten long edge of bias strip. Clip neck curve to ease tension and also trim bulk of seam away. (See Fig. d).

8 Pull collar away from smock and fold bias facing and seam towards smock. Stitch along neck edge through facing, seam and smock. Keep stitching as close as possible to base of collar. Sew ends of facing to back edges. (See Fig. e). Sew snaps and buttons to back opening. Dress on Brock, over the trousers.

9 Sew felt beret sections together round edge. Very carefully, cut a cross on one side to turn beret right side out. Fold points back and catch down on seams allowance. Stabstitch folded edge of opening. Turn beret right side out. (See Fig. f).

10 Roll strip of felt tightly to form a stalk. Slipstitch to hold roll then sew to centre top. Finally, catch beret to head and hold in place with a couple of stitches.

d

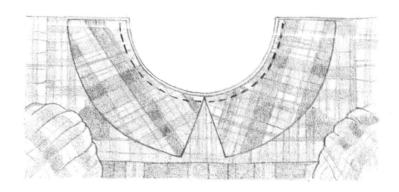

e

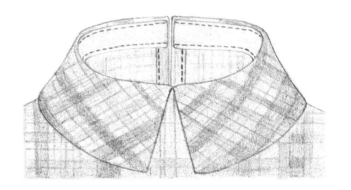

f

GLOSSARY

Appliqué
A fabric design applied to the surface of another fabric.

Basting
A temporary method of holding fabrics together prior to seaming. It is the same as tacking (see below).

Batting
A sheet stuffing used to add softness or padding to an article – similar to wadding.

Bias binding
A strip of bias-cut fabric used to finish neck edges on small-scale dressmaking or to make casings.

Butt
Bring edges together so that they meet but do not overlap.

Casing
A channel or hem open at both ends through which elastic or tapes can be threaded.

Circumference
The distance round the outside edge of a circle.

Close
Finish sewing a seam. This is generally done by ladderstitching a seam on the right side after stuffing a skin.

Diameter
The distance across a circle measured through the centre.

Ease
Fit curved edges together when sewing a flat seam.

Edge stitch
Sew on the right side of an article as close as possible to the edge.

Embroidery thread
Six-stranded cotton for embroidering facial details and monograms.

Fibre fill
Manmade or synthetic stuffing for animal and doll bodies.

Finger press
Open seams under finger pressure.

Gather
Draw up fullness by using two rows of long running stitch.

Grain
Lengthways warp of fabric. It lies parallel to the selvedge and should be lined up with the arrows on your patterns.

Ironing
Smoothing the fabric with a sliding back and forth motion using the weight of the iron to smooth out wrinkles.

Nap
Downy surface of materials such as velvets, velours and corduroys. Care should be taken to determine the direction of the nap before cutting.

Notch
Cut small pieces away from the inside of a curve of a seam allowance to prevent puckering.

Pivoting
A technique used to stitch corners using a sewing machine. Stitch to the turning point leaving the needle in the work, then raise the presser foot on your machine and pivot the fabric on the needle. Lower the presser foot and continue stitching.

Pressing
A shaping and flattening technique achieved by lifting and lowering the iron on to a particular area, usually under a damp cloth.

Seam allowance
The width of the fabric between the seam line and the cutting edge.

Sheet polyester
A manmade batting.

Tacking
Long running stitch used to hold fabrics together temporarily.

Template
A firm shape used to draw round.

Topstitch
Stitch on the right side.

Trim
Cut away excess material from a seam.

Wadding
A sheet stuffing similar to batting.

STOCKISTS

UK
Beckfoot Mill
Prince Street
Dudley Hill
Bradford
BD4 6HQ

Fluffy Fabrics Ltd
28 Tribune Drive
Trinity Trading Estate
Sittingbourne
Kent

Oakley Fabrics
8 May Street
Luton
Beds
LU1 3QY

Ridings Craft
749 Bradford Road
Batley
WF17 8HZ

USA
Dollspart Supply Co., Inc.
The Teddy Works
5-15 49th Ave Dept 2714
Long Island City
NY 11101

AUSTRALIA
Craft Plus
89 Latrobe Terrace
Paddington 4064

Melbourne Street Arts and Crafts
Centre
146 Melbourne Street
North Adelaide 5006

NEW ZEALAND
Handicraft House
37 Orange Avenue
Penrose
Auckland

Forty Two Handcraft Supplies
42 Marine Parade
Paraparaumu
Wellington

Write to the above addresses for
details of their mail order service and
catalogues. Remember to enclose a
stamped addressed envelope.

INDEX